Designing Games Meant for Sharing

This book talks about the importance of social mechanics in games and how these mechanics evolved over time to accommodate new technologies and new social contexts. It looks at the innovation happening in the field of new-age social games, discussing in detail what has been learnt from designing for the younger generation, how these findings can inform game design philosophy and how this can be applied to game development more broadly.

Part 1 of this book provides a brief history of games as social interaction and discusses the differences between online and offline social gaming. Part 2 covers Facebook social gaming and design lessons from first-generation social games. Part 3 introduces design philosophies for the hyper-social genre and includes an important chapter on design ethics. Finally, Part 4 looks ahead to the future of social games and how game designers can incorporate learnings from this book in their own work.

This book will appeal to game designers and students of game design looking to learn how to apply learnings from social game design in their own games.

Ioana-Iulia Cazacu is a Game Designer at Mojiworks Limited.

Designing Games Meant for Sharing

Ioana-Iulia Cazacu

CRC Press
Taylor & Francis Group
Boca Raton London New York

CRC Press is an imprint of the
Taylor & Francis Group, an **informa** business

Designed cover image: Eleanor Sadie Eady

First edition published 2025
by CRC Press
2385 NW Executive Center Drive, Suite 320, Boca Raton FL 33431

and by CRC Press
4 Park Square, Milton Park, Abingdon, Oxon, OX14 4RN

CRC Press is an imprint of Taylor & Francis Group, LLC

© 2025 Ioana-Iulia Cazacu

ISBN: 9781032322971 (hbk)
ISBN: 9781032322872 (pbk)
ISBN: 9781003314325 (ebk)

DOI: 10.1201/9781003314325

Typeset in Palatino
by Deanta Global Publishing Services, Chennai, India

Contents

Part 2: The beginnings of social gaming

Part 3: Social game design for a modern audience

Contents

Acknowledgements

I want to acknowledge all those who contributed in their different ways to my accomplishment of writing it, because it takes a lot of perfect circumstances and support from people and it goes far beyond just my work and passion for the subject.

I want to thank my partner Oscar, who has always supported me in everything I ever did and who has patiently put up with me reading aloud every single chapter of this book multiple times to make sure it all made sense. His patience, expertise and candour have gone a long way to make this book become a reality.

I want to thank my family for supporting me in my endeavour to study and pursue games even when this was a difficult road to take. I want to thank my brother, whose love for games was passed down to me and who, with infinite patience, taught me how to play games and let me win on so many occasions just to cheer me up. I would not be here to tell you about this topic if he hadn't constantly fuelled my love of games since I was a very young child and I am very grateful for our shared common interest.

I want to thank my friend Ellie, who has been one of my biggest cheerleaders since the very beginning and who has so graciously accepted to create the wonderful artwork for the cover of this book. Her incredible talent and hard work have always been a source of inspiration to me and I feel incredibly lucky to have her work on the cover of something I wrote.

I want to thank those who lent their thoughts to this book in the form of interviews: Andra, Jen, Matthew and Patricia, whose insightful words add so much to the contents of this book and who have opened my mind to so many avenues through our conversations.

I also want to thank Will, who not only asked me to write this book but also supported me every step of the way in the publishing process, always being incredibly excited about the work and supportive of my ideas.

Last, but not least, I would like to dedicate this book to my late grandparents, who, even though they never really understood what I did for work, never hesitated to listen to me with open hearts and excitement for seeing me love something so much.

Introduction

We live in a time when the internet is one of the most prominent social tools; some of us, especially Gen Z and younger, cannot even imagine a world in which we are not connected by the grand network of wires that is the online world. This space is a marvel of engineering and science, and with time it evolved to be its own ecosystem far more complex than some would have initially imagined. The internet is a place for all kinds of activities, a place for people to connect and create community and yet much of this ecosystem is still unknown or misunderstood. Social media predominantly is a place where the rules of regular social interaction had to be reimagined, and all of this was a journey of discovery for developers and users alike. As different social media platforms rose to fame and faded away with time, the way people treated their online lives and personas changed. We are currently in a state where online and offline identities blend and influence each other in a way we have not really seen before. In my experience as a social games designer for the past six years, I have had the opportunity to observe this audience through the lenses of the games I've worked on, and the proof of this shift in behaviour is overwhelming, especially after the 2020 pandemic.

As game designers, we feel maybe that we have finally managed to build enough seniority as an industry to be able to tell with more certainty what designs and characteristics make a good game and in some ways we do. But the defining characteristic of the games and tech industry is that we are in a perpetual search for innovation. Until very recently, the ever-evolving nature of games has been predominantly dependent on hardware, and while that trend will continue, current circumstances suggest that the evolution of hardware will slow down until the very next boom, which will possibly be quantum computing. Until then and even beyond, innovation will come from refining the way people use the devices we have and working on the experiences they offer.

The social potential of games has fascinated me from very early on in my career, far beyond my love for MMOs and MOBAs as a player I was captivated by online communities discussing games on forums, the parasocial relationships between streamers and their followers and even the kind of discussion that a simple game of backgammon would facilitate between my elderly relatives. I always knew games to be social in some way, even if they weren't inherently multiplayer, and thus when the opportunity arose to work on a book, I knew that this would have to be the topic of it.

This book is a collection of all my learnings as a designer, as a player and as an observer of people making conversation, spending time and building memories while playing. It is also of course about how we as designers can encourage social behaviour in our games. I am hoping that for anyone who reads this book, the information new and old will be at least shown from a different point of view, one that can help each reader to come away inspired and wanting to make their own games more social. After all, the value of the things we enjoy is always doubled by sharing it with someone we love, and games are no different.

Part 1

Games have always been social

chapter 1

A history of games as social interaction

Imagine this: it's 2500 BCE and you are a merchant at one of the many markets in Ancient Mesopotamia. In a quiet spell of the market, you and other merchants might decide to start playing a game while also discussing the state of commerce. All manner of people have been known to enjoy this kind of pastime and you are of course no different; after all, the Royal Game of Ur (known to you most likely by a different name) has really spread far and wide and enjoys popularity even beyond the borders of this region. Something occurs to you as you arrange the pieces on the board ready for play: although you have played this game hundreds of times it never feels like you are playing the same game over and over again. As you face off against your opponent and start to play, you both interlace your conversation about current topics with little remarks about the game strategy and then it hits you: the game itself is just a conduit for social interaction. Sure you could have the same conversation without playing the game, but the simple act of playing gives you both an activity to bond over, and the conversations seem to flow differently. The same game played in complete silence would not be as entertaining.

Looking at today's society we are not much different from the people in Ancient Mesopotamia playing the Royal Game of Ur. Our means of connecting have changed a lot and so have our games, but the basic desire to connect with others has stayed the same. Human desires and needs are pretty much universal and have remained more or less unchanged throughout history. Learning from the past is of course crucial when it comes to any kind of innovation, but how we approach this can radically change the results we end up with.

Virality

When we examine history and try to learn from it, it's easy to overlook the details that don't translate one to one into our current lived experience. Many terms have emerged in game design in the past decades that describe phenomenons as we see them in relation to video games, but sometimes these phenomenons have existed long before video games and definitely before we had words to describe them.

DOI: 10.1201/9781003314325-2

For example, the pieces and boards for the Royal Game of Ur or similar-looking games have been found throughout the Middle East and India (Tam, 2008). This means that the game resonated with people so much that they took it with them on their travels and taught others how to play. In modern game design language, the term for this phenomenon is "virality".

Virality is essential for multiplayer and social games, be they physical board games or video games; this is because they are limited to being played with other people. Apart from being a great method for the game to gain popularity, growing through virality has a host of other benefits: players will feel more attached to a game they play with friends, they will have fond memories of it and they are more likely to associate said game to social interaction, meaning they will in turn recommend it to others. And this is of course not a thing exclusive to this digital era. If we go back to the example of people playing the Royal Game of Ur, we would probably see a similar story written with a different pen. If your merchant friend showed you the game and taught you how to play, you would be more likely to try to get your own copy than if you just heard about it around the market. Similarly, today a recommendation from your favourite Twitch streamer weighs a lot more than a targeted ad because you trust the influencer and respect their expertise. A recommendation from a friend is even more valuable because it's curated to your specific tastes in games. Even in circumstances where you might be a little sceptical about the game recommendation itself, the relationship between you and the person recommending the game is more likely to lead to you at least giving the game a proper try before you dismiss it. This means that a lot of people who would not otherwise be drawn to the game for its intrinsic value might end up playing anyway for the social value.

Our means of sharing our favourite games with the people we like has changed a lot from ancient times; we can communicate across the world in seconds and video games are ready-made and easy to purchase online. But the desire that drives one person to convince another to play with them a game they enjoy has remained unchanged.

The social contract

Social and multiplayer games rely on the agreement between the involved parties to uphold a certain kind of closed group social contract. The term "social contract" (Shand 2015) is derived from political discourse and it refers to an implicit agreement to cooperate as part of a group in order to receive certain benefits in return. However, in this case, we use this term to refer to the tacit agreement between parties to follow a specific set of softly enforced rules, that while they might not be the letter of the law, they affect our adherence to the group. The way this contract is enforced is through social obligation, which is here used to refer to the way people may feel the need to act in specific ways in order to please others they consider friends. The term "obligation" here is not used to suggest the person responding is in one way or another reticent to doing these things, and it does not equate to terms like "peer pressure", instead it's about the intrinsic need we humans feel to please those we like through our actions.

A game can encourage through its structure the establishment of such a social obligation in order to establish long-term social play. Because this kind of dynamic can be overused it is important that developers use this in good faith and sparingly, so the players feel in control of how often they interact with others but can still see the clear benefits of doing so.

Let's take, for example, Dungeons & Dragons (D&D) and how the game uses the social contract to its advantage while also being mindful of the kind of effect it has on players. Firstly, D&D requires at least two people to play, a Dungeon Master (DM) and a Player Character (PC), though realistically the game is made for larger groups. The two sides of this structure must be present for the game to take place; a DM without players cannot proceed and neither can players without their DM. If the PC party is larger than one (which in most cases it is), all players must agree to join the game before the party can proceed with the adventure. If one of the PCs can no longer join the group on a regular basis, they need to make an agreement with the DM and potentially with the other players about what happens to their character; the same goes for someone new joining a running campaign. D&D (and other similar tabletop roleplaying games [RPGs]) uses a couple of design techniques that enforce the need to uphold the social contract in the group that it is played in.

- **Asymmetric gameplay:** In D&D each person has a class, and while one player could theoretically go through an adventure by themselves (provided the DM accommodated them), the strength of the game comes from the interplay of classes. Suddenly the issue of "John can no longer make it on Wednesday evenings" turns into "What are we going to do without a rogue?" Players are more likely to find a scheduling solution because the gameplay is more balanced and more interesting when the party is balanced. Similarly, the players are more likely to try to get others to join if they are looking for another class to join their party. The wonderful subtlety of asymmetric gameplay in Dungeons & Dragons is of course that it's all in the hands of the DM who can make decisions and adjust the difficulty and the nature of the quest to match the active players.

- **Accessible format**: Although D&D is one of the more in-depth RPG systems out there, it still retains an impressive level of accessibility. You could argue that the books are a significant expense for those starting out, but a single copy can be enough for an entire group and it offers as many possibilities as the DM can dream up. Aside from the obvious investment in the source material, all players really need are pens, paper, dice and an active imagination.
- **Leverage power players**: The DMs of D&D (and really any tabletop RPG) are often the power players of the game. They know the game inside out, they are more likely to buy auxiliary material, and they are very likely to convince others to try the game. This works great for D&D for a few reasons. Firstly, it makes the game less intimidating for new players; if their DM knows a lot about the game, then they can worry less about the subtleties of the game and focus on learning the basics. Secondly, it helps with the initial financial barrier to entry; your DM likely owns all the materials the group needs to play and others can just join. Last but not least, the DM has every intention to make others enjoy the game because a campaign is as much a reflection of their performance as a DM as it is a reflection of the game itself.

D&D has lasted through the years, and even though its popularity has risen and fallen, it still remains a cultural touchstone when it comes to tabletop RPGs. This is because D&D evolves with its audience; the game you get to play today is not the same one as when it was first released in 1974, and this is not only due to the new editions of the rules. D&D encourages player intervention and player-made rules; homebrews can take any shape and may even choose to ignore certain aspects of the game to make it more interesting for the group playing. This, in addition to keeping the game fresh, allows the player to adapt the context of play to the dynamic of the group, establish the boundaries of play and what everyone wants to take out of playing. In the case of Dungeons & Dragons and other tabletop RPGs, it's put to those involved how often they meet, what the expectations are when turning up at the gaming table and what is the amount of involvement one must have in order to be part of it. This flexibility allows the players to form a social contract, that in this case is easier for them to uphold because it's expressly tailored to the group by the members of said group.

Social reengagement

Much like the Royal Game of Ur, multiplayer and social games rely on other people being active participants in order for the game to offer the intended experience. This means a couple of things: firstly, if the player can't find someone suitable to play with them, the game will not take place and, secondly, the quality of the experience is highly reliant on the quality of the relationship the player has with their gaming partner. At first glance, this model seems to have some very strong disadvantages working against it, and yet time and time again throughout history it has been proven to work. This is because the same things that seem to hurt it can end up helping it succeed.

One of my earliest memories of people playing games together is of my grandfather and his neighbour playing backgammon and chess outside in the garden during the summer months. The way they played games was a bit like a ritual: they would finish a long day of work outside caring for the animals or tending to the orchard. After that, when the air was cooler and they finished their day's work, they would get together over a glass of plum brandy, gossip, and play. In other words, the game was there as part of a routine and the social interaction gave them an excuse to play; this is what we call social reengagement.

This type of reengagement relies on the participants making a habit out of playing the game together, and it works very well as a method of getting people back to the game. To be able to take full advantage of social reengagement, the game in question has to become part of this kind of social contract between people, which means that the parties involved have a tacit agreement that they will follow a pre-established set of rules, and in this case a pre-established routine. There is nothing to stop one player from ditching the other, but they do it out of an implied agreement, and if one party bails, the others will get upset. Becoming part of someone's social ritual is challenging, especially in a world with so much content, but once achieved, players will return to the game organically and will remind each other to play. To understand more about how this can be used to our game's advantage, we need to take another look at history.

Party games are exclusively social; their purpose is to engage people and entertain them during parties and gatherings. Unlike classic board games like Chess and Go where the agreement to play is between two people and the rules are very strict, party games have looser rules and they can be played with a large number of players. Take charades for example, the only immutable rule of the game is "do not speak while miming". As long as the players keep that rule, the rest of the game can be rearranged to accommodate the group that is playing. For example:

- Players can keep score or not, which lets them decide how competitive they want the game to be based on the kind of social situation they are in.
- Players can be split into teams making this more of a group activity or they can play as individuals in a free-for-all style making the game a lot more focused on the individual.

- Players can use syllable and number or word conventions or not, which allows the group to tailor the game's difficulty.
- Players can choose to play with a single category of subjects or go broad, which not only affects difficulty but it also lets the players tailor their game around their specific interests.

In the case of charades, the low barrier to entry and the flexible rules that can accommodate any number of players made it easy for the game to initially establish itself as the game to play at parties in early 19th century France. The historical context in which a game becomes popular is very important; if charades did not exist already and got invented, now you might see how it would struggle to become popular, but because it is an already widely known established game people still play to this day. This is because the game has been passed down through generations as an activity suitable for gatherings, so social reengagement is very strong. Even if a group of people have not played the game together before, they are very likely to have played it with others, and the simple act of getting together reminds them of the game and so the cycle continues.

Sociocultural context

Entertainment and its value as seen by the public that consumes it has always had a strong connection with the state of society. This has many facets and it expands beyond the topic of games to other kinds of entertainment:

- Appealing to current societal desires
- Accessibility in the current social context

Appealing to current societal desires doesn't always mean the game has to directly address current events but rather it has to fit in the current view society at large has. For example, Monopoly has been a popular board game for family nights for decades now, and throughout time countless reskins of the original concept have been created. But what really created such a long-lasting legacy for this game? After all, the game itself is almost entirely governed by chance; even the dominant strategies are not much to go off of in Monopoly, almost like the game is telling the player that winning in the game of fortune is ultimately determined mostly by luck and not smart investment.

The case of Monopoly is interesting. The original creator, Elisabeth Magie, created The Landlord's Game as a piece of social commentary. She designed the game to be a representation of her views on the ill effects of monopolism and presented in it novel ideas about how the land tax was a way to solve this issue. The goal of the game wasn't initially just acquiring wealth, but when Charles Darrow agreed with Parker Brothers to publish a game "very similar" to Magie's Landlord's Game, the goal of the game shifted to creating a monopoly instead, hence the name. While Darrow is largely recognised as having been falsely credited as the original creator of Monopoly, it's worth pointing out that the changes he made to the overall goal of the game might not have been entirely unrelated to the success of the game over time. Making a statement about society in a game can be powerful and gather a lot of backing from people who are of a similar mindset, but the dream of becoming incredibly rich and powerful is a desire that can be sold to a lot more people (and has been for years under the guise of the American dream).

Accessibility in the current social context is also incredibly important, and video games of today are simultaneously incredibly easy to access and incredibly inaccessible. On one hand, we can argue that free-to-play mobile games have changed the way that we think about consuming entertainment and that even those that invest nothing in entertainment itself have access to some form of it. On the other hand, video games are still for the privileged who can pay the initial price of owning the hardware necessary to play in the first place. When creating games that are meant to be played socially, making them as easy to access as possible is a huge deal because the preposition to play a game turns suddenly from "let's play this game together" to "can we both afford to play this game". There are many ways video games have dealt with lowering the financial barrier to entry, one of the more obvious examples being couch multiplayer. Fighting games, for example, have proven that this model not only has staying power with franchises like *Street Fighter* or *Mortal Kombat* being still popular 30-plus years after their original release, but they are also incredibly financially successful. The crucial part of couch co-op is that once one of the players is convinced to play the game, there is no additional barrier or cost for their friends to join them in playing. This works brilliantly because it both offers access to the game to those who would otherwise not be able to play it, but it also functions as a promotional tool, for example, if the friend enjoys the game and can afford the buy-in price they are more likely to purchase it themselves. Of course this type of co-op is limited to players being in the same place at the same time, which does not seem to be very in keeping with the kind of communication and social lives we have nowadays. This is no doubt a reason why more modern games have started to move away from this multiplayer model or include an additional online component that allows players to join each other from anywhere as long as they have access to the internet. In Chapter 3, I will talk in more detail about the advantages and disadvantages of online and offline social play and how they can be used to achieve different results.

The living ruleset

Oral transmission of rules and players' involvement in determining what the game ultimately becomes has been a key feature of games in the past. Oftentimes players will experiment with their own house rules in order to make the experience more entertaining for the context they are in. This might be seen by some developers as damaging to the integrity of the game rules, after all, players are not designers and they have not spent all this time learning about how to create the perfect system. But in reality, players have an advantage in this scenario: they know what the audience wants best because they are the audience.

Some players will always try to push the boundaries of what is possible in a game; some of them might even resort to cheating in order to get a different experience the game considers to be not intended. The real way to make sure that players can bend the rules to their desired experience and still keep it fair for everyone else is by encouraging the upholding of the social contract during the game. For example, if we think about a homebrew rule for D&D the only people who need to agree to it and uphold it is the group playing that specific campaign. Similarly, if we are talking about a player using banned cards in a Magic: The Gathering tournament, which is something that all tournament-goers have agreed not to do, we can rely on the social contract and expect others to report the player for cheating.

Trading card games (TCGs) are an interesting example of what I like to call a "living ruleset". A lot of physical games use revisions and reskins to update the ruleset of the game, but TCGs have a unique quality that helps them be a lot more flexible: they are built to be modular. The ruleset for such a game is comprised of multiple layers:

- The basic table layout and goals
- The abilities of individual cards
- The banned and limited lists

The table layout and goals are the glue that binds together the rest of the game. While not immutable, this part of the rules would be the last to change in order to accommodate new play styles and cards. Take, for example, Yu-Gi-Oh. In the 20-plus years it has been available in the West, the goal of the game has not changed at all: the player must reduce their opponent's life points to zero before their opponent has the chance to do this to them. The table layout hasn't changed drastically either, though a couple of new card slots have been added to accommodate the new mechanics described on new cards. The speed and dynamics of the game, however, have changed entirely since the first iterations of the game. In the beginning, the game was less focused on card synergy and had a lot more back-and-forth with the players relying on buying themselves time to summon their powerful monsters. In the most current meta, however, players aim to win in as few turns as possible, linking actions in the same turn and using card synergies to get extra actions. The reason why this is possible is because a significant part of the rules for Yu-Gi-Oh are contained by the cards themselves. While the broad-stroke rules for the game are less flexible, cards have incredible flexibility. As long as the original rules are kept in mind, there is a whole world of experimentation that can be created for each card; this includes introducing new mechanics, changing number balancing and adding new lore and flavour text. And if a new card turns out to be more powerful than originally expected and starts affecting the competitive aspect of the game, the creators can ban it or limit that card's usage.

But how does this really affect the social component of the game? Well, at the core of a living ruleset is always the game's community. In many ways, to be able to shift and evolve with your audience is something that requires a lot of effort, but due to the modularity of this system and the ability to easily add and subtract for it, it can help in theory to have a game that keeps the people interested engaged by catering to them with small changes. Of course there are also drawbacks to this system as in most cases; over time some of these systems become so complex that new players struggle to join, especially if they do not have someone to teach them the ropes. Ultimately, when a game desires to be long-lived it has to choose between entertaining its existing versus its new customers at times, and the living ruleset can help to independently address different parts of the demographic.

Social-added value

It's fair to say that even the most commonplace experiences can be made memorable in the right company. This is because the connection between people adds social value to whatever experience we are talking about. Games benefit a lot from this added social value, which can take a couple of forms:

- Playing games as a bonding activity
- Using games to find like-minded people
- Using games as a status symbol

A great example of a game that takes advantage of all forms of social-added value is chess. The game is played at a casual level among friends, and while the practical goal of the game is outsmarting your opponent and winning, the social goal of the game is to be a bonding activity. The players know each other and while the mechanics of chess force the two players to be in opposition, the social aim for this is to become closer friends by the end of the game. At a more macro level, local tournament-goers have a stronger desire to win than those playing a friendly match; in this case, the practical goal stays the same, but the social goal changes. Players are looking for others who can match their skill level and while they might not end up winning the tournament, they are sure to make new acquaintances they will keep running into should they continue to compete in tournaments. Those competing in national or even interna-tional chess tournaments have a different social goal: they use their ability to play the game as a status symbol looking to prove to the other chess players that they are the best.

All players, from novices playing friendly games to national champi-ons battling for the number one spot, play the same game, they abide by the same rules and they have the same practical aim to the game, but the social-added value for each of these people is completely different. The game achieves this with an easy-to-understand but hard-to-master game-play because it allows players to have different levels of involvement with the game mechanics. The basic rules of chess are in theory very simple: each piece has a moving pattern, and each turn players can capture an opponent's piece and eliminate it from the game. The win condition is a bit more vague but still pretty simple to understand: if a player's king is in immediate danger of being captured by the opponent and they can't make any valid moves to escape, the player loses the game. The wonder-ful thing about chess is that these simple rules create a huge possibility space for different strategies and outcomes. As a result, mastery of these mechanics comes from understanding the complex repercussions that a single move can have over the entire game, anticipating the opponent's moves and crafting a strategy.

While player skill seems to have a direct correlation with the type of social involvement a player seeks, it is not actually that straightforward; they are instead two separate aspects of the game that drive each other. The complexity of the game makes the competitive sphere for the game more meaningful for those who are very skilled, but whether a player competes is ultimately driven by their desire for a particular type of social interaction. It's perfectly plausible that very skilled players will never join tournaments because their goal is to use the game as a bonding activ-ity with their friends. Inversely, a prodigy might bypass the casual play phase entirely and learn more about the game with the sole purpose of competing.

The demand for games as entertainment is now bigger than ever, and more games see social play as an attractive prospect. It's important for us to analyse the games that came before to see what attributes made them successful. Even though the games we make today are very differ-ent from their precursors and they aim to be liked by a modern audience, the techniques they use can be adapted to the current environment. In the next chapter, I will talk more about a person's adherence to a group, how that influences their choices and view of themselves and how this ultimately translates to in-game behaviours.

chapter 2

The person, the group and the game

It is undeniable that people around us change the way we express ourselves and with time they might even change the way we see ourselves. The
self is a complicated concept that gets formed around the circumstances
in our lives, circumstances that are most often brought on by society or
the people around us. Similarly, when building a video game identity or
persona there are a multitude of factors that contribute to it, including the
type of game we are playing, the mood we are in and last but not least the
people we are playing with. The conversation of identity in video games
is thoroughly explored in games academia, as the topic is a gold mine for
revelations about the psyche of the player. In this book, however, we focus
predominantly on multiplayer and social games and I think there is lots to
be discussed and discovered about the intersection of the virtual identity
of someone and their social identity.

The self: What is identity?

Our identity is composed of many parts that determine who we understand ourselves to be and inform the way others see us and communicate
with us. The subject of identity is most often brought up in day-to-day
society when we discuss someone's belonging to a specific group, therefore it is actually incredibly difficult to separate the identity of a person
from their social integration based on their characteristics or beliefs. But
in this case, identity refers to the person's view of self and has less to
do with how society categorises the individual based on their identity.
For example, being a nerd is an integral part of my identity: I have nerdy
hobbies I engage with, most of my friends are also nerdy and if I were to
see an ad that said "All nerds assemble, new loot dropped in the shop" I
would most likely identify with that tagline and check it out. Being a nerd
is how I define myself to be, but it is also a handy shortcut for other people
to address me and other people with the same interests as me. There are
also characteristics that I cannot change about myself that are part of my
identity. I consider myself Romanian, I was born there, I hold a Romanian
passport and I'm engaging in the culture even though I have lived away
from my country for many years. The fact of my ethnic background will

DOI: 10.1201/9781003314325-3

never change for me even if my citizenship situation changes; as far as I am concerned being Romanian is part of my identity.

Depending on the situation I am in, these different aspects of my identity may or may not matter to others, but they still remain part of my identity. This is not to say that identity is inflexible or unchanging, on the contrary, our view of ourselves changes with every passing event. It is likely easiest to look at identity as the individual looking from inside to the outside, this is why often there can be discrepancies between what society understands us to be and what we actually identify with. The source of truth in this case is of course always the individual themselves, but in extreme cases the individual might have to compromise in order to comply with society's taxonomy. In this case, there is a difference between someone's "true identity" and their legal identity.

Someone's legal "identity" is a kind of social fingerprint, the way governments distinguish one individual from another; this is what terms like "identity theft" refer to. The two types of identity are interlinked: both our perceived identity and our legal identity are there to not only serve the purpose of categorisation in society but also to attribute civic rights and obligations to each one of us (things like having the right to vote or the obligation to follow the law). There is a very vast conversation to be had about how one influences the other, but for the purposes of this book, we will only concern ourselves with identity as perceived by the person. I recognise there is also a conversation to be had about impersonation online and how the online identity of a person can be manipulated and the impact it has, however, I will only lightly touch upon the subject as it pertains to video game identity because the subject of online impersonation and catfishing is beyond my area of expertise.

In a way, identity is a very difficult term to define because it refers simultaneously to what brings us together with others (e.g. belief, culture, hobbies, personal convictions, etc.), but it also refers to the way in which the unique combination of these factors makes us individuals. There is also a conversation to be had about expressing one's identity and to what degree the external expression influences the true identity. This subject is particularly relevant when we discuss both virtual and social identity, so I will explore the topic further as we delve deeper into the subject.

But how does understanding identity influence the way that we design games? I believe there is an additional benefit to understanding this beyond scholarly curiosity, and that is building empathy. When building personas that we then use to guide our design process we are creating a profile of a player, the archetypal person that enjoys our game. It is fundamental to understand, however, that beyond all those similarities that we list, there are actually millions of different people with different identities, and ultimately none of them will experience our game exactly the same. It is also worth being conscious of the intersections of identity that may make the game more or less appealing to people from certain groups and why that is. Last but definitely not least it's about offering a range of options for self-expression, being as inclusive as possible and understanding the importance one's identity plays in their interaction with others.

The group: Social identity

You might have previously heard the term "social chameleon" to refer to a person who is highly aware of social cues and uses their observations to "blend into" the group or social situation (Ellemers et al., 2002). The desire of humans to fit within society goes beyond the fancies of modern life, they are instead fundamental to us surviving and thriving as a social species. It is because of this need that humans developed such an acute sense for reading emotions in others based on facial expressions, so much so that we start attributing the same emotions to other creatures like cats and dogs. It is this desire to fit in that drives the individual to alter or conceal things about their identity in order to match the group's "standards" and adhere to the social contract. Not everyone's identity is equally impacted in a group, however. The accepted behaviours in a group are determined most commonly by members who have a position of leadership or a more dominant personality. This means that each member of the group has to decide what kind of adjustments they would need to make in order to fall in line with the group, and it is up to the individual to determine what value the adherence to the group has in relation to expressing their own identity. More frequently than not, there are multiple factors that determine how much value someone places upon being part of a group versus their ability to express themselves, or how much one will abide by a group due to prior commitment even when their own identity might be affected negatively in the eyes of society (Ellemers et al., 2002).

The position a person has within the group also affects how much they are "allowed" to deviate from the norm of the group, with those in positions of power generally being let off the hook for things others would not be.

When a person is part of a group that becomes part of their identity, they might end up with specific roles and "responsibilities" and they might suppress or amplify certain parts of their personality in order to fulfil their role. The group has a huge influence over the individual and depending on the group this can be both positive or negative. Knowing this, games can use the social contract to encourage behaviour in players, but we have to do it ethically and treat their audience with care, maybe even protect them from toxic group dynamics that could emerge inside the game. We will explore this topic later in this chapter as well as in the following chapters.

The game: Virtual identity

Virtual identity refers to the self-perception of the person as it is constructed in a virtual space, in the case of video games this means both the expression of it as the avatar and the behaviours imprinted on the avatar by the player while they are controlling it. This identity is formed within the parameters of the game, but it is in this case separate from the players' real identity and it is not bound by any common traits between the player and the avatar. People may choose to reflect their own looks and beliefs in this virtual identity if the game allows, but forming a virtual identity is more about the connection of the player with the character within the confines of the game than it is about similitude. This does not mean, however, that any player can "identify" with any character, but rather that a character the player identifies with could be anyone.

Oftentimes we see the argument of games as immersive spaces where the character is an extension of the player used erroneously or in bad faith, to suggest that diversity is not necessary, that whatever the character on screen might be or look like the player will identify with it just by the nature of controlling that character. This is of course a bad argument especially when used against the diversity of playable characters, mostly because the subject of identifying with the character on screen is a complex one, but also because if it does indeed not matter what the character on screen presents as, then an argument cannot be made that it makes a negative difference to include more diversity in the way these characters present.

Representation in video games is a very important topic, especially when discussing virtual identity and how it forms, as the limitations of the game world help the player form a vision of themselves that they resonate with and subsequently that affects their engagement with the game. Note that we are not talking about the character being a one-to-one virtual copy of the player or even a close approximation, instead it's about the emotional response someone has to the character. Virtual identity does not concern itself only with the games where the players can build an avatar. However, the ability to do so exposes the subtleties of how players go about building an identity in a video game. While part of it is about the way the character looks, it goes far beyond that to include the way the character acts in cutscenes or even how "skilled" or powerful they are in relation to the non-player characters (NPCs) of the world.

Depending on their preferences or goals, players might adopt different styles of customising an avatar as:

- A virtual representation of how the player sees themself (most commonly this representation is idealised to a greater or smaller degree)
- A window to the player's "real self" (this may be aspirational or experimental for the player if they feel like their appearance does not match their true self)

- A "roleplay" avatar that is unrelated to how the player sees themself (this is often done to explore the boundaries of what is possible in a game)
- An avatar that is meant to resemble an already-existing fictional character (this is called cosplaying)
- Shortest route to building an avatar (most commonly using default presets)

Building the avatar goes beyond the way the character looks, it is also about how they interact with the world, their abilities, the choices they make in the story, etc. Players do not have to adhere to one style of avatar or another. This might vary depending on the players' mood, the game they are playing and, as we'll see later, the people they are playing with as well. But regardless of what this character looks or behaves like, the player will use their ability to influence the way the avatar presents in the game in order to identify as that character inside the video game.

Even in games where you control a predefined character, the player creates this kind of bond with the avatar they are controlling. Sure it might be Mario who gets told that the princess is in another castle, but as far as I am concerned, while playing the game I am the one being told that, I am the one playing the game and passing the obstacles and enemies on the way, I am Mario.

Virtual identity becomes quite a grey area for games where there is no avatar, for example, *Tetris*. As a player I get to control the falling blocks, but I am not one of those blocks in the same way that I was Mario in the previous example. But even though the through line is not so obvious as it is when an avatar is present, the ability to control what happens in the game and the way the player approaches goals and challenges constitutes some form of virtual identity as well however loosely that term might be used in this case. Deciding what actions are and aren't characteristic of my playstyle and identifying with the goals and limitations of the game means that I get to identify as the entity that controls the game.

Figure 2.1 illustrates how virtual identity relates to the player's identity and the avatar.

What parts of the game contribute to forming this virtual identity is a topic still explored by academics and this is where the concept of the "hybrid" identity comes up in literature. The concept here is that there is an added layer between the player identity and the virtual identity that, while it emerges in the context of the player playing a game, is ultimately independent of both the player and the player-character (Boudreau, 2012). In theory, this suggests that identity can stem from other non-game-related activities that concern the "character", which includes but is not limited to other player's perception of them. This may include things like fan art and fan fiction or even discussions on different forums about the character. It then suggests that this character starts to have a "life of their own" and

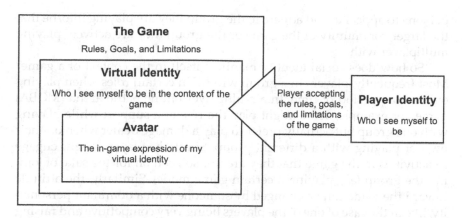

Figure 2.1 How virtual identity relates to the player's real-world identity

a reputation of their own, and even though their existence started with the player interacting with the game, the existence of that character is no longer bound to either the player directly interacting with that character inside a game or even the game being actually played. We notice this most commonly with streamers when their avatar becomes to the viewers both a representation of that player and their own entity. Similarly, we notice a similar phenomenon in the case of tabletop role-playing game (RPG) shows like Critical Role where the characters created by the players become no longer bound by either the creator or the ruleset of the game being played.

Most commonly then we notice that this hybrid identity emerges from the social interaction of the gameplayer either with a community that is watching or with a group that they are playing with. And while the study of such an identity started with massively multiplayer online role-playing games (MMORPGs), it extends beyond even the realm of games into social media (Boudreau and Dixon, 2013) where we use our ability to present and catalogue content in order to play with self-expression and which ultimately can create an identity that is neither attached to us as the user or our persona online but rather the perception of all those factors in the eyes of other people.

The chatbox: Virtual social identity

Considering that virtual identity is a version of the player identity, it follows logically that there is a virtual equivalent for the social identity of a person when we present ourselves online in a medium that is meant for social interaction (Wood and Solomon, 2009). In the case of social media, the user will use facts about themselves to appeal and be accepted by those who follow them (be they real-life friends or not). Similarly, when someone plays a game in a social context, they will build their game persona to appeal to and adhere to the group they are playing into, be that the larger community of the game or the group they are actively playing multiplayer with.

So how does social identity manifest itself in the context of a game? Most frequently, players in a group will fill in certain roles when playing over a long period of time. In a multiplayer online battle arena (MOBA) game, for example, some might play the role of a support while playing with one group but actually prefer to play a damage dealer when on their own or playing with a different group. Similarly, players might engage in activities in the game that they are not so keen on for the sake of joining the group (e.g. playing a certain game mode). Similarly, the attitude toward the game can be changed by someone with a dominant personality, like in the case of one of the players being very competitive and raising the stakes and competitiveness of everyone else in the group.

Virtual social identity is very similar to the real-world group identity but much like the virtual identity of the player it gets shaped by the rules and limitations of the game. Especially in the case of asymmetric gameplay, players need to negotiate positions inside the group structure the game requires in order to succeed.

Take for example a game such as *Keep Talking and Nobody Explodes*. In the context of the game, one of the players must be the one who tries to detonate the bomb, while the other must be the person with the manual. Based on the role, the players must use different skills and take on a certain attitude towards the goal to succeed (i.e. the player with the manual must to the best of their ability describe the action to be done and the player with the bomb must listen to the other's advice). Regardless of which of the players tends to be the leader in any other situation, in order to succeed they must work together and abide by the roles that the game is assigning to them. Similarly, when playing a game like *Among Us* players are given the role of either crewmate or traitor. The game dictates these roles and the players must play according to their goals by either fulfilling tasks or causing chaos and murdering crewmates.

What is more interesting about these games is that in order to have the intended experience, the individual as well as the group must abide by communications rules that the game cannot strictly enforce. If instead of explaining how the bomb works, the player sends a picture to the other player, then the game would not be any fun; if the people who have been murdered in *Among Us* speak out loud and point at who killed them, then the game would be over very quickly. In multiplayer games where the gameplay is intentionally asymmetric, the virtual social identity refers not only to the dynamic and hierarchy of the individual inside the group and their role in the game but also to the goals of the group while playing the game and the restrictions that get imposed on each player. This can be done either in a hard way by limiting what each player can do or in a soft way by incentivising everyone to behave according to the ruleset in order to have the desired experience.

This, however, does not only apply to asymmetric gameplay, even though it is easier to observe in those kinds of situations. In the case of *Counter-Strike: Global Offensive*, for example, where all players have access to the same kind of weapons and resources, the virtual social identity is more fluid; players are still operating within the boundaries of what the group goal is, but the structure of the group is formed organically based on preference or ability. One of the players might be better in close-quarters combat while another might have a better aim, so in order to achieve the goal of the game, groups must distribute their players wisely and use a game-wide strategy, which is what ultimately imposes the role upon the individual.

In a way, we could argue that this is still a way for the game to softly enforce a structure. If winning requires strategy, then any roles inferred from that are a way for the game to suggest a structure. It is, however, a bit of a blurry line. Some games might start off with no predefined structure or strategy, but over the course of the games' lifespan, the community explored the mechanics and emergently found that certain formations are more efficient than others. For example, *League of Legends* started off with a roster of champions the players could play and the three-lane structure, and while certain characters had different characteristics that made them more suitable for one play style or location, the game did not enforce any of this in a hard way (e.g. by not allowing players to choose characters with similar make-up or abilities). As players explored the game, however, they attributed these roles to the different champions, and with time any deviation from this was considered "wrong" even if the game did not enforce it to begin with.

The main difference between the real-world social identity and the virtual social identity is their relationship with the self. The person's real-world identity determines their social identity as part of the group, however, because the game has the added goal of a win state, the virtual social identity ends up influencing the player's virtual identity more than the other way around (Figure 2.2).

The community: Fandoms

Being part of a large group is in theory not too dissimilar from being part of a small one, however, the reason why I think it's important we consider fandoms separately is because with large numbers of people, the result is rarely a homogeneous fandom. More often than not fandoms behave like a collection of groups that may or may not have much intersection with each other even if they nominally like the same thing. Take for example the *Dark Souls* fandom. There is a group of people who play the game for

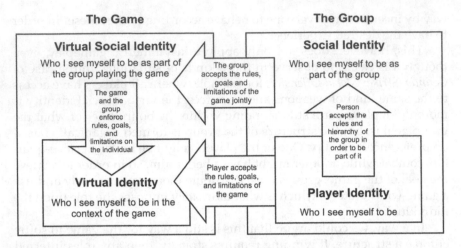

Figure 2.2 How the group affects a player's real-world social identity and their virtual social identity

the challenge and take pleasure in the high skill execution required by the game; there is another group of people who enjoy the game for its fantasy and lore speculation. The two groups overlap to some degree both in terms of the people (i.e. some people enjoy both the hard gameplay and the lore) and also in terms of how they see one aspect of the game influence the other (i.e. the lore explains why this boss is harder or the difficulty of the gameplay is filling a gap in the written lore). However, the person's adherence to the fandom is not reliant on them enjoying both aspects of the game, even if members of the fandoms might protest otherwise.

The matter of inclusion in the fandoms is an interesting topic to discuss, especially in the context of this chapter that revolves around identity. When it comes to the real-life identity of a person it is the individual who determines what is and isn't true. However, when it comes to adherence to a large group, who holds the truth? If I would like to consider myself a member of the group but I do not meet the "criteria" of said group, am I still a member?

Organised groups have a governing body that decides what are acceptable qualifications for the member of said group (e.g. only engineers can join an engineer association). In the case of small groups, such as friendship circles, the social contract between members covers who is and isn't included with either the majority holding the final decision or the person(s) highest in the hierarchy of the group (e.g. we do not want to be friends with X because they always cause drama). But in the case of fandoms, this becomes very tricky: who has "ownership" over the identity of being a fan? At first glance the obvious answer is the individual; after all, they decide if they like something or not. However, the truth is more nuanced because fandoms are not only about enjoying the content, it is about community. Belonging to a fandom actually means being part of a subgroup inside the fandom; as long as one can find kinship inside the community the amount of other fans the person identifies with does not matter. Take our earlier example of the *Dark Souls* fandom; if I want to play the game for the intricacy of the lore and the speculations around it, and I find community in people who enjoy this aspect of the game, it should not matter that I don't actually enjoy the high difficulty very much and that I asked friends to cooperate in order to get over the most difficult challenges in the game.

Adherence to a group or a fandom becomes even more interesting when the overall effect on the perceived self-identity of the members is somewhat negative, yet members choose to remain part of said group out of some other perceived benefits (Ellemers et al., 2002). A great example of one such instance is adhering to the identity of being a "gamer". Because gaming and tech started as niche activities and the enforced gendering on video game consoles sparked by advertisements started with positioning the Nintendo Entertainment System (NES) in the boys' toy aisle in the 1980s, we know that even to this day identifying as a gamer can have negative facets. On one hand, there is the matter of being questioned by other members of the community and the gatekeeping, the perceived idea that gamers look and behave a certain way and have poor social skills, and that gaming is an infantile activity meant only for children and those who have nothing better to do. The perceived view of the community seems to exclude a lot of its members. So then the question becomes why do those members still want to adhere to it. The answer is: strength of commitment. For a lot of people the medium of games has been a form of comfort they have engaged with for a lot of their lives and the gamer identity is how they can express that to the world.

Why is player identity important?

Apart from being a fascinating subject to discuss, understanding player identity is quite a fundamental pillar in creating a game that captivates and immerses the player. When it comes to building a personal virtual identity, the player must be able to project themselves in some way inside the game. This means that we as creators of games must offer our target audience the tools they can use to build this identity and keep the limitations within the realm of the player's expectation. The gap between what the player expects the boundaries of the virtual space to be and what they actually are can negatively affect the way in which a user can build their identity. In cases where the difference between the player's expectations and what the game offers is too significant, the player can no longer suspend their disbelief and therefore immersion is broken.

The willing suspension of disbelief is what helps the user accept the rules and limitations of the virtual space (Böcking, 2008). When talking about literature of theatre, for example, the suspension of disbelief is about engaging with the content knowing that it is fiction but embracing it as "real" for the duration of the play or the time reading a book. We do this to emotionally immerse ourselves in the storylines and empathetically respond to what we are consuming as if it was real. In games, willing suspension of disbelief is even more complex. This is because not only does the player need to accept the "fiction" presented to them, but they have to act as part of it. This is when virtual identity comes in to bridge the gap between what is real and what is not.

Another important angle to consider when it comes to our identity in online spaces, such as a social multiplayer, is how the boundaries of the game and the way we see ourselves in these places affect the way we play and interact with others both outside and inside the game. The Proteus effect (Yee and Bailenson, 2007) is the phenomenon in which the user behaves differently based on their constructed virtual identity. This means that as we get to see ourselves in a certain way inside these spaces we might feel emboldened to act differently than our usual normal response. The literature suggests that not only do players feel more confident when being represented by an attractive avatar but these behavioural changes ultimately translate to our in-game interaction with other players, meaning there is a degree of transfer to how they feel about their real self when controlling such a character. If the goal is to create spaces where players can be themselves but also make sure the game fosters a friendly social atmosphere, it is really worth considering how virtual identity spills into people's lives via the Proteus effect and how we can use this knowledge ethically to foster healthy social relationships inside and outside the game.

How we perceive ourselves in online spaces: Interview with Andra Ivănescu

I met Andra Ivănescu during my games design studies at Brunel University London. As my games studies lecturer on matters of sociocultural issues, she really opened my eyes to seeing the world of games content in a completely different light. Since then Ivănescu has done some amazing work with the university and in academia in general and is now in the beginning stages of some incredibly fascinating research on identity and avatars, which I believe to be a perfect addition to this chapter.

Andra Ivănescu: My name is Andra Ivănescu. I'm a senior lecturer in game studies at Brunel University London and the program lead for the Undergraduate Games Design course here. I am a ludomusicologist by training and part of a larger research group that also organises the ludomusicology conference and co-edits a book series about video game music and sound with Intellect. I'm a member of the British DiGRA [Digital Games Research Association] board and for the purposes of this, it's probably important that I also co-lead the Living Avatars Research Group.

Ioana-Iulia Cazacu: Thank you for the introduction. Before we delve into more in-depth topics, I was thinking we can talk a bit about your personal history with games and especially playing games with other people.

Andra Ivănescu: I started playing really young and my first memories of video games are actually of playing them with other people. I was at my mom's friend's house, where her son and his friends would play games together and I got to join. Whenever the grown-ups got together, they would send us to the kids' room and we would play, mostly fighting games. If I remember correctly we played quite a lot of *Mortal Kombat* at a very inappropriate age. There was also my uncle who is 9 years older than me; although we never actually played together, I played his games and it feels like we have in one way or another shared our gaming experience that way. Because of him, I played games like *Prince of Persia* and *Civilization* and I think it's interesting to talk about the social communities around games that don't always involve playing together, because it has always been an important part of my experience. I remember sharing video game magazines and demo CDs at school with the boys in the class. Also even though I never really did much of it myself, the Romanian experience in the late '90s was definitely going to internet cafes and playing together in that way.

Ioana-Iulia Cazacu: I vividly remember my older brother spending his pocket money to go to internet cafes. That was where he would scope out what games were interesting so we could pirate them and play them at home. I am very glad you mentioned the social experience around playing non-multiplayer video games because I believe games unite us even when they're not specifically made to be played "together". I also resonated with what you said about your uncle influencing your taste in games because I had very much the same experience with my older brother.

Andra Ivănescu: It's interesting and to some degree I believe it's something quite special to look back on a time when the internet was difficult to access. Nowadays the shared experience of playing games feels quite different, especially that I get to see it from an adult's perspective. But those moments of socially sharing games still exist. I see it happening at events when I get to play or even just watch students play. The same experience of standing around, commenting on what is happening on the screen, and just having a good time where the game being played is the main event. I remember a Halloween event when we played *Lovers in a Dangerous Spacetime*. We projected the game on a massive screen. Some people in the room were in fancy dress because they were heading off to Halloween parties afterwards, and all of us were sort of commenting on what the people playing should be doing in the game. It was such a lovely experience.

Ioana-Iulia Cazacu: I think that is a very important experience for those studying game development, and hopefully they also go on remembering that feeling and trying to accommodate that feeling in their games later on in their careers. Speaking of your work at Brunel University, that is also where you started your research in avatars. Can you please tell us more about your goals for this research and how did that all come about?

Andra Ivănescu: I'd love to! It all started as part of the Brunel Research Interdisciplinary Lab initiative. Under this interdisciplinary initiative we hold workshops that aim to bring people together from across the university, people who wouldn't otherwise meet each other essentially and talk about things and find shared interests. What we found through these discussions was a shared interest in avatars. We each had aspects of this topic that we wanted to know more about that we found to be insufficiently studied in our fields. Coming from a game studies background I already knew quite a lot about avatars, because in our field people have been studying this for a couple of decades now if not longer. I was particularly interested in the voice of the avatar. That was my starting point because I felt like sound and voice had not been explored as much as other aspects of the topic. And because of this shared interest, we found our group: a neuroscientist, a cognitive psychologist, a philosopher, and a couple of lawyers. In coming together and exploring what we would want to do we realised our aim was to essentially put all of this research together and do something truly interdisciplinary. Essentially we wanted to see how all of the research from these different fields fits together and we discovered there are actually a lot of difficulties in doing so. To give you an example, something we realised from the very beginning is that we used terms differently, and you can imagine that makes all communication challenging.

Ioana-Iulia Cazacu: Interesting. Do you have an example of that?

Andra Ivănescu: I have the perfect example because this is one of the things that drew us in and is a thread that goes through our entire research now. When a neuroscientist and a cognitive psychologist talk about ownership, what they mean is how we, as people, see extensions of ourselves as embodied. So they would talk about things like the rubber hand illusion where you have your hand in a rubber glove and hidden, and they see a rubber hand being stroked, even though it's not your hand, your brain perceives it as your hand being stroked. So, there are aspects of our brains that can see the sort of parts of our bodies represented on screens or in VR [virtual reality] environments, as being us or as being our extension in various ways. This is not my field so I'm trying to summarise what everyone else has been explaining to me for years.

When sociologists and people from game studies think about ownership we jump straight to talking of identity. How do we identify with an avatar? What does that mean? Are our identities projections? Are they part of ourselves? And other conversations stemming from that come to mind. Do men prefer to play female avatars because they're experimenting with identity? Is it because they just like to look at a female body? Is it because they can find in-game advantages? There are all of these different ways in which we think about identities and how people like to play in virtual worlds, right?

Then you move this idea to the philosophers and the lawyers and they ask things like: Who owns it? Who has the legal rights over the avatar? And that is a good question. Who has the legal rights over things like the representations of ourselves? Is it us or the game developers? And the more we delved into it we got to discussions about regulation, things from Raph Koster's Declaration of the Rights of Avatars to T&Cs [terms and conditions] we sign every day, that sort of thing. Because it is ultimately a discussion about human rights so there are legal issues to consider. And remember that all of these questions and discussions stemmed from this single word: ownership.

Ioana-Iulia Cazacu: I'm assuming there's many words like that and that you spend a very long time trying to discover what those words were so you can be on the same page. I find your goal of understanding the subject of avatars and identity from all these different angles fascinating. It's really about going beyond the knowledge in your immediate field and connecting the dots. It's something I've noticed happening a lot more in game design recently as well. We reached a certain maturity with game design that we're starting to embrace knowledge beyond the obvious inspiration like product design, UX design, and film and TV. It's great to see more psychology incorporated into design or even things like human biology or law. These new ways of looking at games have very interesting results and I think are a good sign that we are becoming a lot more purposeful and less intuitive driven as a discipline. But continuing with our conversation about your research, what would you say is your favourite part of this project?

Andra Ivănescu: It's the different perspectives and the fact that we get to explore how people understand virtual worlds differently, and the broader implications thereof. It was because of looking into fields like neuroscience and cognitive psychology that I started to change my approach when looking at certain concepts. To give an example, game scholars lump virtual worlds together, (be them text 2D, 3D or VR), but our brains perceive those differently and they react accordingly. That changes how we understand things like identity in video games and avatars.

Ioana-Iulia Cazacu: I see, there are of course certain advantages to thinking of them as similar when designing these experiences, it allows us to apply our knowledge more broadly to different projects, but I can see that when it comes to research like this that distinction would allow you to delve deeper.

Andra Ivănescu: Yes, there are practical reasons to lump them together but I think we also want to resist technological determinism. We don't like this idea that technology drives how we do things and how we engage with things; we like to feel more in control.

Ioana-Iulia Cazacu: I agree, and another layer to this is looking into how different people interact with that technology based on who they are. We see a lot in the younger generation having a different attitude around technology and the internet, so is it possible that they interact with the same media in some different way because of who they are? I don't really like to focus on age brackets and demographics because that can quickly go into the wrong direction. But you can tell when someone was born closer to when smartphones came out; technology and the internet are second nature to them, they treat it as an extension of themselves.

Andra Ivănescu: Do you think it's a question about digital and gaming literacy?

Ioana-Iulia Cazacu: To some degree yes. But I am always surprised by what the younger generations do and don't know. I would say my generation and older generations had to tinker with tech a lot more to get it working, and that kinda made us more aware of how things worked in the background. But with everything being so well designed nowadays, anything that falls just outside of this well-designed bracket becomes really obscure to those not used to things being a bit crappy and broken, and there's so much choice out there as well that they don't need to put up with it. This is not lamentable by the way, just interesting to me. I think we should always aim for more inclusive, better designed experiences, but these highly polished surfaces do a really good job at concealing the mechanisms inside it all. Much like a mechanical watch or a smartwatch, the smartwatch is more powerful, but the way in which it works is a lot more obscure, so it becomes more about what the watch can do for you and not how it does it.

Andra Ivănescu: It's interesting for sure. What I noticed in my students is a fetishisation of difficulty and a fascination with souls-likes that partially stems from them being used, as you said, a certain type of very designed experience. Something I hear a lot from these students, who are maybe 18 or 19, is that they see those kinds of games as the pinnacle of difficulty. Because they don't have experience with old arcade games that had difficulty as part of their make-up (because that is how they made money). So it's interesting to see how that gaming experience and your past experience with tech can actually change the way you perceive a game as well.

Ioana-Iulia Cazacu: Exactly, and the whole identity of "gamer" that people ascribe to themselves, how do they experience things differently because of the social pressures of that role. Because it really influences what people allow themselves to like and dislike out of a desire to fit in.

Andra Ivănescu: I love that you bring this up because this whole thing of identifying as a "gamer" is again an issue of identity and an issue of belonging to a specific community. I find it fascinating as someone who knows a lot about gaming communities and how gamer identities form to go out and explore those things in the wild, as it were. I've been asking my students the question of "Do you think of yourself as a gamer?" for about seven years now, and it's always fascinating not only to see their answers but their reaction to being asked. I think as time goes by there are less negative associations with the term "gamer" but there are still social pressures around it, and in general women tend to describe themselves as gamers less frequently even if they play games. It's also a question of what games are considered "hardcore" or worthy enough to "grant you" that title. Casual games are an obvious kind of game that people don't see as "real games", but some others earn similar vitriol, cosy games are another example. It goes beyond difficulty and complexity to "decide" what makes a game a "real game" for "real gamers" as most things like this are entirely decided by the social zeitgeist and it is still quite gendered I must say. The games preferred by women seem to be seen as far less "credible" in that way.

This happens less than it used to, but you still see the same kind of gatekeeping and elitism persisting. You see people playing the same kinds of games when they end up on a games course. I mean, *GTA 5* is ten years old and that is still the most popular game that has ever existed in all of my cohorts.

Ioana-Iulia Cazacu: I think this is fascinating and if you don't mind me going off script a little bit, I would love to discuss how you see your students look at the topic of being a gamer and having to prove themselves in order to fit into this little identity box. How do you see them navigate that, especially on a games development course? Do they do things to prove themselves to each other?

Andra Ivănescu: I find a lot of these things a little bit more insidious than they used to be but trying to prove themselves is definitely still a thing even if it's not overt. The conversations around "playing the right kind of games" and "playing for the right amount of time", that sort of thing; basically everything that Adrianne Shaw[1] wrote about in 2012 to 2015.

I saw this outside of the games course as well. I recently taught a master's class on avatars to students from a different department. I asked them the same question I ask my students: "Are you a gamer?" And if I recall correctly, only two people in the whole class said yes. But when I went around in discussions, they were saying things like "Yeah, I just play on my mobile" or "Sometimes I play this casually" and it took me pointing out to them that those are also video games for them to acknowledge that they play regularly. They somehow had the idea that these were not "the right kind" of video games.

Ioana-Iulia Cazacu: I wonder to what degree that is because of gatekeeping and how much it is because they want to distance themselves from the perceived negatives of that identity.

Andra Ivănescu: It's a bit of both and let us not forget this is still also very much gendered. It's a question of "who gets to dictate what are the right games" and "what different people must do to 'prove' their identity". I had a student who did a very interesting dissertation a couple of years ago that looked at peripherals and the gendering of that side of gaming, with a famous example being those cat ears headphones on one side and the sleek black look on the other. The subtleties of why certain gaming peripherals are marketed to different demographics and why is part of selling that "gamer aesthetic". What they found is that oftentimes not only was there lack of women in the creation and distribution of these but often lack of humans. There's a lot of robots in the advertising for all this and it's so widely spread that we hardly even notice.

Ioana-Iulia Cazacu: The topic of proving your gamer identity through hardware is interesting for sure, and I am certain there is lots to explore there that we are not able to go into right now, but I am hoping it will spark interest in readers to go out and look into it more.

Andra Ivănescu: I hope so, I think there is so much to talk about when it comes to this topic.

Ioana-Iulia Cazacu: Circling back to your work on avatars and in-game identity, could you tell us more about the stage of the research you are at?

Andra Ivănescu: Currently we are at that exploratory stage, so we don't have any findings per se to share. At this stage where we're sharing the experiences with each other from our own fields and putting those together like puzzle pieces to then be able to test these in a much larger experimental setting.

Ioana-Iulia Cazacu: So this stage is about writing down your questions and looking at them from all the angles?

Andra Ivănescu: Yes we are building a common literature and applying for funding. We want to create an experimental study that includes the particularities of research in all these fields: the neuroscience aspects and lab testing, the more traditional game studies ways of testing in the virtual world, and then passing it all through that legal filter.

Ioana-Iulia Cazacu: I am not very familiar with this type of research and the steps required. Would you be able to tell us a bit about how you go about structuring your research?

Andra Ivănescu: Truth is every research project is different and we are still working on what we want to do and how it will all work. The thing we know we want to do and the thing that is most difficult is putting together these different methodologies. What the cognitive psychologists and the neuroscientist wants in this case is to conduct research in a lab doing brain scans and monitoring people's brain activity. Then what we want on the games studies side is a virtual world setup and we haven't decided whether to use a pre-existing game or build one ourselves. We care a lot about the ability of people to create a likeness because it changes everything about the study. We want to test all different parameters: gender, race, etc. Studies like this have been conducted before, but they were all testing these aspects individually, but what we want to do is to merge it all together in a series of tests and look at all the data together to see what new information we can find.

Ioana-Iulia Cazacu: I wanted to dig a little deeper into this topic with you because while it's obviously not exactly the same, we do a lot of user research in my line of work. And one of the things that I find very interesting about it, is that when people know they are observed they behave differently. I was curious about your point of view in this and how you conduct research of this type where you aim to see the player's real behaviour.

Andra Ivănescu: I think part of the answer is that you can't, really. But part of it is about time because people do forget that they are being observed.

Ioana-Iulia Cazacu: Interesting. I never thought about that, but I guess it makes sense that you just fall into your own habits after a while.

Andra Ivănescu: Pretty much.

Ioana-Iulia Cazacu: When you do these types of studies, do you find that self-evaluation is useful? Do you have certain ways of dealing with self-evaluation in this case?

Andra Ivănescu: I mean there are layers to that, part of it is how you write the questionnaire. There's a lot of research into how to develop a questionnaire that gives you valid answers, that doesn't have leading questions, that evaluates what you're trying to evaluate and all of that. But self-evaluation is always tricky. You have to account for certain things that will always be skewed, for instance, one of the classic things that game psychology knows is that we're really terrible at evaluating how long we play for. We're just famously really, really bad at it. We can go into discussing the magic circle and all that. But this is just one example of the kinds of things that you can account for because it's something that we already know happens and has been tested and proven already. There are many other such details. And then there is a discussion about the statistical evidence, and how you look at those questionnaires statistically, particularly if you're doing more quantitative research and bringing in other methods. Depending on what you're trying to test, whether you're going off of metrics that become about sample sizes and statistical significance.

Ioana-Iulia Cazacu: I think there's a lot of overlap between the kind of user research done in development, and the research that you do in academia. The techniques are the same but they are applied in different situations. For us it's a lot more zoomed in on a specific element – "Do you like this or that" or "Do you understand this" – and that is mostly because we focus on the solution of how to make something better. It's interesting looking at academia because it's more about the why and less about the what. That's not to say that they don't feed into each other, after all the goal for both is ultimately to understand human behaviour all the same.

Andra Ivănescu: Yes, I believe that is fair to say, they are similar but not the same.

Ioana-Iulia Cazacu: I had another question I just recalled from one of our previous conversations. We talked a lot about our online persona especially as it pertains to social media. I wanted to know what your thoughts on the online identity influencing our offline behaviour? Does the online self influence the offline self you think?

Andra Ivănescu: To me the answer is very clearly yes! That is for a few reasons, partly because we use our online personas to experiment (most of us at least). We use them to play around with our view of ourselves. in the case of anonymous personas we use them to experiment with boundary-pushing that would not be acceptable in the real world in various ways. That kind of experimentation teaches us about our own identity and our own behaviour. So I think that's a definite way in which our online personas influence us as people going about in the real world. But I think there's another way, that is maybe not as direct but just as important. Through our online personas we interact with other online personas, and the behaviour and that social environment is very different from a non-virtual environment.

And I would even say there's a less known third one that we don't talk about very much, but research into MMORPGs and virtual worlds in general has shown us that the design of virtual worlds affects the behaviour of people in them. They do so through the affordances of a game, the things that it rewards. However they are constructed, all of it affects behaviour. But this doesn't only apply to MMORPGs, it is broader than that, and I think it very clearly applies to social platforms. The design of anything from Reddit to Twitter and what their algorithms value affects what people say and what people see. So yes, designers and corporations can affect our online personas, and that translates into real-world personas as well.

Ioana-Iulia Cazacu: I believe that to be true as well, and that is why design should always be done in good faith. One of the things that I like to say a lot is that it's not enough to want to be ethical, you have to actively want to not be unethical. Because that's definitely one of the things I notice in some developers, is that they don't even know how much power they're holding. For example, a designer would probably not think "I want to make a game that is so addictive it's gonna make people forget to eat", but we use so much psychology in game design that something like that can happen regardless of intention. So yes, a hundred percent I stand by what you said regarding the power developers have in influencing someone's virtual and real persona. It was also very interesting to hear about the different levels of interaction with other people and how we test the boundaries of social interaction. This is especially because of something that we've seen a lot with our audience which is predominantly Gen Z: they tend to build platform-specific personas that they carefully curate. Sometimes they even have more than one on the same platform choosing carefully who can see them and how they come across to that selected group. And this is all very interesting and mysterious to me because coming from my generation I am used to having social media as my online representation pretty similarly across platforms, but for them it's much more fluid than that. For example, my cousins are Gen Z and they have so many accounts on Instagram from which they send me pictures and the vibes are always very different. One of them is " Growing up together" meme-type stuff and in the other one it's about vibes and "I'm a cool teenager". It's all very precise and aesthetic. Although I have to say it feels less fabricated than some of the stuff we used to do at the height of the Facebook likes craze; they are kinda unfiltered but they just keep certain aspects of themselves to share only with certain people.

Another thing you mentioned was about experimenting with identity and testing the boundaries of that. I was thinking that in a tabletop RPG for example you are sort of limited by what you can get yourself to say out loud, and that is maybe unsurprisingly a pretty big deal. Unless you are a very experienced player or a very good actor you might find that pushing your boundaries that way it's more uncomfortable. But obviously, virtual worlds have a level of abstraction to them. I have an avatar most likely and I am not doing these things myself, I just make my avatar do it, although I am the one pressing the buttons and making it do something.

Andra Ivănescu: Yes there's also something called the Proteus Paradox.[2] This suggests that changes in an avatar's appearance influence people's behaviour sometimes in quite drastic ways. For example, if you are taller, you are more assertive. If you perceive yourself to be more beautiful or your avatar to be more beautiful you are more social with other people. And all of this is part of what we want to do with the research group, as well, because all of this research is about games at the moment, but does this not apply to our other online personas?

Ioana-Iulia Cazacu: Of course, that is a great point. Especially in a world where as we said there is so much room for crafting a persona, with filters and careful aesthetic curation of content.

Andra Ivănescu: It's fascinating to explore the relationship between not only changes in our appearance online but how those changes reflect personas. In a real-life social situation we would talk about frame theory,[3] a concept explored in sociology many decades ago, which suggests that depending on the social situation and our perception of it we behave differently – we use framing to understand and respond to communication. But of course, this reaches a new extreme online. It can be taken a lot further than in real life.

Ioana-Iulia Cazacu: I suppose it is because of that layer of separation we spoke about. Something that I find also very fascinating is the relationship people have with streamers and that parasocial relationship. Because you feel like you know that person, but obviously you know what they want you to know. And you might feel like you are able to count on their authenticity, but obviously we know that sometimes it all just blows up and we find out things about these people and we feel betrayed or lied to. But at the end of the day it's an act, where they intend to present their most likeable traits to the world.

Andra Ivănescu: Yes and especially with professional streamers this is not just an act but their job and that dictates in itself certain behaviours that will just get you more viewers.

Ioana-Iulia Cazacu: That is a very good point. Their livelihoods depend on you being liked or hated, is more about what brings the money in.

Andra Ivănescu: Yes and entire careers are built on being hated and reviled. Just getting people to shout at you.

Ioana-Iulia Cazacu: But obviously being that sort of public character is nothing new, for example, one of my favourite historical figures is Diogenes and he is known to be a philosopher and sceptic, but his whole thing was basically just being an inconvenience to everyone. In the end I guess that is one way to get your name remembered.

Andra Ivănescu: Yes, it is.

Ioana-Iulia Cazacu: Speaking of history is actually a perfect segway into the next set of questions I had for you. Previously in your career you have looked at nostalgia and how it influences us when we talk about games. Can you tell us more about it?

Andra Ivănescu: Sure. I love discussions about nostalgia. My research is specifically about popular music and games. But nostalgia obviously goes broader than that, and there are many things that I like about nostalgia. But a lot of it I draw from Svetlana Boym's *The Future of Nostalgia*. Her point is that there are two types of nostalgia: there's reflective nostalgia and restorative nostalgia. Restorative nostalgia just wants to bring back the "good old days", it sees the past as this glorious thing. And we can see this running all the way from things like "Make America great again" to " None of these series are what they used to be" or "The first Pokémon was the best one". And reflective nostalgia, that which sees the past with good and bad. And you can linger in that longing, but you understand that it's a longing for a time in your past perhaps or a certain aspect of the past that you enjoy but not necessarily all of it. You can see its flaws. And again it's not about denying the longing for that something but it is just understanding the context in which that thing happened and how our vision of it is distorted by all other factors at play in our lives.

Ioana-Iulia Cazacu: I think what we play at pivotal moments in our lives shapes our tastes for the rest of our lives. For me that was 16–20-something, but what I find fascinating in how it's not the actual game but the memory of how that game used to "feel" to play, and the way how all those games were so much better in my memory.

Andra Ivănescu: I think that's one of the keys to nostalgia right because it's not really a longing for the past but a longing for our memory of the past. Sort of how we perceive it now, not even how we perceived it then. And we know quite a lot about memory, which plays into this fact that we can invent and rewrite memories very easily. But this longing is sort of almost by definition seen through rose-tinted glasses. And it has always existed. If you look at the history of retro gaming as soon as you had a second generation of consoles, there were people longing for the first.

Ioana-Iulia Cazacu: Of course. I also think that as an industry we are not progressing as fast as we used to, mostly by the nature of the medium. We had a boom and we're now at the point where we're starting to slow down, to a degree I assume that is also why people say games are getting "worse" or "more of the same". I think it's very interesting to talk about how this is not only nostalgia for the content, but this nostalgia for how rapidly things progressed, the jumps from one year to the next were incredible. I'm not saying things are not improving but the ways in which we are progressing are more subtle.

Andra Ivănescu: I think that is true to a degree but the thing that is very interesting about all this is that people don't only long for how things used to be better but also how they kinda used to be worse in a way, or I should say different. Nostalgia makes people also crave the imperfections of older technologies. The most obvious example that I always give is musical. You will often hear music from the Fifties (in a film or game) and it will always have an added vinyl crackle effect, even if you can get a crystal clear recording of said song. That's because it signifies things, it evokes a specific time, it makes it sound "authentic".

Ioana-Iulia Cazacu: So how does nostalgia play into our memories of playing games with other people?

Andra Ivănescu: It's interesting to see 18-year-olds playing games selectively from gaming history and I notice there's a nostalgia. It's kinda fabricated by the media, and it's very different when it's your own memory of these games. It's not just nostalgia for a period of design or the imperfections of the console, but it's nostalgia for that time in your life and the experience you've shared with people.

Ioana-Iulia Cazacu: I definitely found that even just with other people that played a game in the past, you "compare notes" and realise how different you experienced something, sometimes even mis-remembering significant parts of the game. Or another hilarious example to me is when people remember a game being a lot better than it was because they played it with friends. People remember how "fun" it was to play something not how technically competent a game was, sometimes even bad games end up being loved because of the hilarity of co-op.

Andra Ivănescu: Absolutely and it's also very common for people to remember enjoying something that at the time they didn't, pushing to defeat a difficult boss that made you angry is a very common example. Nostalgia gives us not only a view on who we used to be and how we interacted with others, but it's also about the here and now, how do we filter all of it through the prism of what we know today.

Ioana-Iulia Cazacu: This is why I like to say that games are there for us to create memories around them, but there is so much more to how we remember games than the actual content you engage with, people remember emotions, they remember a time in their life and they remember their friends. I really enjoyed our conversation today, and I hope so did you. As a closing remark, what would you say is probably most important for people to leave this interview with?

Andra Ivănescu: That video games are profoundly social and while that is often the source of many of the problems we see in gaming communities and even outside of them, it's also what makes them a great force for good and for change. Knowledge is really important in this process so I like to think of understanding these social worlds and the avatars that live within them as a small step towards understanding ourselves and understanding what we can do with and in games.

Notes

1. Adrienne Shaw, "Do You Identify As a Gamer? Gender, Race, Sexuality, and Gamer Identity", *New Media & Society*, vol. 14, no.1, pp. 28–44, https://www.ctcs505.com/wp-content/uploads/2016/01/Shaw-2012-Do-you-identify-as-a-gamer.pdf.
2. See Nick Yee, *The Proteus Paradox: How Online Games And Virtual Worlds Change Us—And How They Don't*, Yale University Press, 2014.
3. See Goffman Erving, *Frame Analysis: An Essay on the Organization of Experience*, Harvard University Press, 1974.

chapter 3

Games as a piece of the social puzzle

Many of us know games as a social experience, from playground games to hypercompetitive online experiences there is a through line that connects it all: we yearn to share games with those around us. This could be because play is a social activity at its core. Many species aside from ourselves display playful behaviours, especially in the early stages of development. Animals, like humans, use play as a social tool, to bond with their kin (Power, 1999), and while the games we talk about are far from the play-fighting that lion cubs do, I believe the needs we are trying to fulfil are similar.

I would argue that playing tag on the school grounds with your friends during lunch breaks fulfils similar desires as joining your friends online to play a game of *League of Legends*. As per previous examples, we can observe how play can take many forms and appear in different shapes over time, but the psychological itch they scratch is very similar to other games that came before. In this chapter I will explore the different ways in which games are social, from playground games to board games, from split screen to online; and I will highlight the unique styles in which these games engage us socially.

Physical games

When it comes to non-digital games there is an array of activities that classify as play, from board games to team sports to playing make-believe. Physical play is something that humans have been engaging with for a very long time. Because of the activity we can observe in other species, we can assume that the desire to play is an innate one, and, beyond socialising, play is a way in which the child experiments and discovers the world.

Because of how broad the definition of play is in this case it's worth using some specific terminology that divides the play into two different types: ludus and paidia (Frasca, 2013; Caillois, 1961). The two terms are not at all new in the world of games academia, but in order to make this clearer in this context I will briefly explain what these terms mean. Ludus is the rule-oriented side of play, whereas paidia is the imaginative side of play. Because of their nature, the two appeal to different human needs and desires: ludus is rational, it's about understanding the systems of play and experimenting with them, while paidia is emotional, it's about

DOI: 10.1201/9781003314325-4

self-expression and experimenting with the boundaries of creativity. In this way, a child playing make-believe is entirely about paidia, while two people playing chess is all about ludus. But the lines are not always that clearly drawn between (Jensen, 2013) the two in my opinion and the same game can be interpreted by different people as having a different balance of these two components. These terms are also not limited to physical games, but the way they manifest is delineated in this context. Throughout this chapter, we will see how these two terms are relevant when analysing the ways in which different kinds of games are played in a social context.

Children's play

What is there to learn from observing the way children's play encourages social interaction and establishes social connection? After all, there is no structure to speak of when we are talking about imaginative play. If we think about it, when we are playing make-believe what we are doing is engaging in unstructured role-play. At a very young age, children use play to engage their imagination and make sense of the world. Make-pretend is there to allow the child to experiment with the boundaries of social interaction and mimic what they observe in the world. For example, when children "play doctor" they assign to each individual roles such as the doctor and the patient. In this situation, the kids experiment with their understanding of the different activities that happen in social situations and how they comprehend the social dynamic between the roles (e.g. the patient must listen to the doctor in order to complete the examination). This kind of play is situational and it involves a shared imagination of the same situation; the social interaction between the participants happens with a layer of abstraction, which in this case it's the assigned role.

Another type of social play is based on a common goal, for example, children playing together with Lego or building a sand castle. This type of play is there to help the child understand more about cooperation and compromise in order to reach a common goal. This is where children experiment with their position in a group, working together and negotiating. This kind of social interaction happens with no added layer of abstraction; the child is not playing a role, instead they are attempting to understand what social devices can be used to achieve their personal goals (e.g. if I want to build the best sand castle, I will befriend the child that has the sand-castle-making tools).

While children learn and experiment a lot when engaging in playful behaviour, we know we cannot look at play only in a functional way. Games are about joy and entertainment, they are also about creating memories with other people while bonding over the same activity. When we are young, make-believe is enough to entertain us; in this case the play is pure paidia and there are no explicit play rules. In this circumstance, the children can also experiment with creating their own rules and socially enforcing them.

Past a certain developmental age, kids start showing less interest in playing make-believe. This is often attributed by the general public to a loss of child-like imagination, but what I believe actually happens is that pure paidia is no longer sufficient to entertain us. When we are very young there are plenty of new factors around us that keep us entertained, plenty of things to experiment with and explore, the entire world is new. As we start to understand the world better, however, we find that every-day situations are no longer as interesting to explore, so we instead start fabricating or engaging with further constraints to operate under. This is when structure starts working its way into play.

Ludus is there to offer the participants a goal or a framework; this makes the structure of the game more interesting because it imposes limitations to operate under making even common situations new again. Ludus also implies that the participants are aware of how rules work and the benefit of following a ruleset. In physical play this is particularly relevant because there is nothing to really enforce the players not breaking the rules in favour of having an easier time. Structured play teaches the child about using constraints to increase their enjoyment of a game, and it teaches them about honesty, sticking to the rules in a social context and the effect breaking the established rules has on other people's opinion of them.

Tabletop role-playing games

To me, tabletop role-playing games (TTRPGs) are the natural continuation of child's play, and in a way they share many similar aspects. While often guided by a set of rules that encapsulate the context of the TTRPG and how it's played, much of the memorable experience of these types of games revolved around paidia. In this case, shared imagination play is what the community calls "theatre of the mind". This means that there is a collective effort to imagine the same scenario together, much like in the case of children playing doctor. The roles are there to challenge the player to either explore a facet of their personality, experiment with social roles and responsibilities and/or use the character as a narrative device in order to create a joint story.

The popularity of TTRPGs and the fact that they have persisted over time even though they have ups and downs suggest to me that adults still yearn for the same connection and joy that kids often get from play-ing make-believe. We want to experiment with the boundaries of social interaction, want a reason to act in uncharacteristic ways, and we desire to entertain others with our impersonations and to work together to solve fic-titious problems that have no bearing on our real lives. Paidia is a route to experimenting with the things that societal norms restrict us from doing as members of society and especially as adults. This is not to say that role-playing is solely or even predominantly about expressing hidden desires or doing what society punishes, like in the case of committing a crime for example, instead it is about experimenting with situations that don't for one reason or another commonly occur in our day-to-day lives. And more often than not, this experimentation is the positioning of the self inside a group. Say, for example, I am a very quiet and timid person. When I am playing my character, a charismatic bard who likes to be at the centre of attention, I can temporarily experiment with that social position and see how it makes me feel. This experience can either validate my current attitude outside of the tabletop setting (i.e. I do actually hate being loud and the centre of attention) or it can offer me the opportunity to experiment with the extent to which I want to have that social positioning in my day-to-day life (i.e. I would enjoy being a bit bolder in social situations).

Aside from the paidia of role-play, TTRPGs use ludus to their advantage as well to encourage and structure play. I would split these into two categories:

- Written ruleset
- Table cannon

The written ruleset is the part of the game that is actually designed and delivered by the creators of the game; this contains everything from items, monsters, combat rules, lore, etc. The written ruleset is the set of tools that the group adopts in order to structure their play. The game master or the group might make a joint decision to actively embrace or reject some of these rules, but they are there to offer all the necessary means to create an engaging experience for everyone involved. This is ludus; it is the structure that makes the difference between playing one tabletop or another, and it is how the creator(s) can enforce the game's balancing and make sure playing is fair for everyone involved.

The table cannon on the other hand is a bit more complex; these are all the rules and "known facts" about that specific campaign that have come about through improvisational play and have stuck around long term. This is when a fact starts off being generated by paidia and then later gets installed as part of the ruleset becoming ludus. For example, the druid of the party wants to befriend a band of wolves, but rolls a natural one and in a hilarious role-playing moment the player suggests that they actually cannot tell the difference between dogs and wolves, which leads to them wandering carelessly in the forest and getting frequently attacked. While initially done as an improvisational bit to amuse the other players, it then becomes canon that this character cannot tell the difference between dogs and wolves and therefore every subsequent encounter with wolves will play by this rule.

To give extreme examples, let's explore how a TTRPG would look like as a pure ludus experience and as a pure paidia experience:

Ludus would allow us to roll dice and to form tactics around the rules in order to combat the horde of enemies attacking. Ludus would also need a conduit for the rules, so miniatures and detailed maps will need to be used, and while this likely sounds similar to the experience of some players with TTRPGs there is a fundamental element missing that separates a game like this from its wargaming predecessors: the role-playing. Even with miniatures on the table and everything strategised to perfection, this kind of game would not be the same without the play pretend.

Similarly, if paidia was the only experience, we would not have the structure of the ruleset; instead the gaming experience would turn into something more akin to the joint storytelling people do around the campfire. While captivating in its own way, this experience lacks a focus or goal, turning it from a game to a creative activity.

The combination of the two aspects in the case of TTRPG makes it an engaging social activity. Players are given goals in order to structure and help with their role-play. Dungeon Masters (DMs) are given tools to create a captivating gameplay environment, and both the player and the game master share in the fantasy of the game session , which ends up satisfying both the social needs for collaboration and the sense of freedom that originates in experimenting with playing make-believe.

Board games and party games

Board games are predominantly seen as dominated by ludus. The idea is that while we are engaged with the game, we need to follow the rules provided to us by the creators. The rules in the case of a board game are a lot less negotiable than something like a TTRPG. This is because there is no figure of authority in the case of the board game (like the game master in a tabletop game), instead the ruleset is the authority on what is and isn't allowed. This is mostly the case for games that enforce their rules in a hard way such as chess or Go. These games do not encourage a way of interacting that involves imaginative play, although in theory one can approach any of these games in a playful way if they wish, but the rules must always be followed in order to be considered a valid match of chess or Go.

Games like this satisfy the desire to jointly work on the same problem or compete to solve the same problem, which for a board game is the win condition. Like in the case of TTRPG, as we grow we feel the need for added complexity in the problems that we solve, and this is when ludus comes into play. Oftentimes, board games offer a simple goal but restrict us in the way in which we can reach that goal meaning we need to use problem-solving and strategy in order to reach it.

With a few exceptions, board games are predominantly a social experience. This means that much like children playing with Lego the participants are experimenting with the social rules of working together, negotiating and seeing how they could convince others to help in order to achieve their personal goals or desires. Take for example a game such as Catan. While competitive in nature (each player is trying to be the first one to get to ten victory points in order to win), the players must cooperate and trade resources in order to achieve their goals quicker (build roads, villages or cities) and accrue said points. The ruleset of the game encourages the players not only to strategise on their own and decide what to invest their resources in but because the map is shared among everyone playing the game, and people can "get in the way" of you achieving what you are aiming for, there is a great degree of social strategy involved. Players may try to create pacts in order to prevent the player who is in the lead from winning, or players might try to convince one another of what is the best strategy to apply in order to favour themselves as well. In a game like Catan the other players are "obstacles" to operate around in order to achieve the win state, and problem-solving must involve all parameters including anticipating other people's strategy based on their play and making sure they do not get in the way of you fulfilling your own goals.

A game like Catan relies on the overlapping of goals in order to make the social interaction part of the game strategy and many board games propose some variant of this. Some games give players a joint goal that requires people to strategise together and decide what is the best course of action. Some games have a joint goal as well as personal hidden goals making people choose between what is the best decision for the group versus the best decision for themselves. In any of these situations, it all boils down to negotiation both with the self and with others.

Party games take negotiation one step further. Unlike other board games, party games are meant to be light and easy to understand, with the ability to accommodate a varying number of players. These kinds of games are meant to focus less on the strategy and more on how the strategy affects the "mood" of the people interacting; basically, these games are treated like a social catalyst. But what are party games, are they predominantly ludus or paidia? This is a very interesting question to ask. On one hand, party games are less bound by rules, meaning they rely less on ludus, but on the other hand, they are not about imagination and exploring creativity in the same way that a TTRPG would be. This is I believe when the style of game is determined by the individuals playing. We can interact with the game in a purely mechanical manner and experience mostly ludus, or through the social interaction explore creativity and imagination and experience more paidia.

Although paidia can be freeing, it also requires everyone to be involved in the fantasy. For some players this can feel pretty daunting. In order to encourage social interaction, both board games and party games use the same strategy: the game offers all the context and content you need to play both intact and strategise with each other. This means that fun can be had with less friction or preparation. This style of play is suitable especially when players have different levels of knowledge or involvement regarding the game, and this is why board games or party games are revered as good family activities.

Video games

When discussing video games ludus and paidia work a little differently, because unlike a physical game, which is only limited by the user's interpretation of the rules, the video game creates what is called a "possibility space", which includes all actions permitted by the rules of the game's world (Bogost, 2008). We could even look at it as the video game being limited by someone else's understanding of the rules being set in place. This is also why I believe most video games are predominantly ludus with far less wiggle room for paidia though not entirely devoid of it. While some games specifically encourage creativity and creation (see, for example, sandbox-type games like *Minecraft*), most commonly the paidia experience in video games comes from filling in the gaps in the game's world. This in my opinion plays a role in nostalgia and is why we seem to have a distorted view of what games from our childhood used to be like; there is a lot left to the interpretation of the player be it intentionally or by the nature of the tech limitation. Players might even remember doing things in a game that they could not actually do or they might feel upon returning that the game does not have the same "lustre" as it did when they first played it in their younger years. This is because when we are dealing with a virtual world there is a layer of interpretation of what happens on the screen that creates a paidia experience. This means we are adding details on top of what is presented to us that allow us to be more immersed in the game.

Paidia might also come from interaction with others that is incorporated in the game but where the means of communication were not intended by the developer. To do this players may use systems that are meant for one purpose in a new way. A good example of this is the act of teabagging when a player uses the in-game valid movement of crouching while over the body of a fallen enemy player in order to assert dominance and show disrespect. In this case, the intention of the crouching was to be used in gameplay, the ludus dictates that the purpose of the move is to duck behind cover and prevent being shot, but paidia desires to experiment with the social roles and interaction and therefore players use the crouch to express their feelings in this way.

Video games look and seem to behave differently from physical games, but the way they encourage social interaction is pretty similar. They still use the basic rules of both ludus and paidia in order to encourage the basic exploration of rulesets, identity and social positioning.

Local co-op

Local co-op games are the next logical step video games could take from the multiplayer games that came before in the arcades. Couch co-op also sprang out of technical limitations. The internet was initially designed for slower communication and video games were not seen as an application for it until the mid to late 1990s. Instead, players could connect via LAN in order to play together on PCs, and console games would sometimes offer the option of split-screen multiplayer.

Local co-op has a lot of the characteristics of playing a board game. Players have the ability to verbally communicate and emote with minimal effort since everyone is in the same place at the same time. This means that the "shared fantasy" is very easy to establish; players might discuss what is happening on the screen and riff on each other's ideas. This helps both the ludus part of gameplay with players being able to strategise together and grab each other's attention when the moment calls for it, but it also helps with paidia with the players pointing out the way they understand the world of the game and sharing a joint "vision" of what is happening on the screen.

Let's take for example a fighting game where the players are playing in the same room looking at the same screen. Not only can the player observe the movements of the characters on the screen as they are controlled by their opponent, but they can also observe their opponent's actions in real life. Do they look calm and calculated doing precise button combinations or do they mash the controller buttons randomly? By using both virtual and non-virtual data points players might size up their opponent, explore their behaviour and adopt different strategies. Similarly, however, players might make use of the physical presence to taunt or annoy the other player in order to distract them from gameplay and make them lose.

When playing video games in the same environment, the physical presence of another person helps break away from the limitations of the game. Not only are we able to interact physically with one another, but the fact that the presence in the game is doubled up by the presence in real life creates a space where playful behaviour around the game is allowed to flourish. Modern online communication has many of the same attributes of interacting with a person (i.e. voice and video) and to some degree these attributes can simulate a similar kind of interaction. However, physical presence is more than just being able to see and hear those around us and interpret their behaviours, it's also about the chemical signals our body gives out and how we as a social species respond to them.

Our senses are incredibly powerful tools, and the way we form memories around certain events extends beyond the audible and visual. Everyone must have at some point smelled a scent that instantly transported them back to another place in time, maybe even reminding them of a specific person. Even though we don't initially associate one sense with another in the moment, the brain retains far more information about a moment than we can tell. The satisfaction and desire to be part of a community extends far beyond our need for entertainment; it is part of our survival strategy as humans. It's precisely that we stuck together and cared for each other that we as a species survived and became so advanced. So it is no surprise that hanging out with people and spending time together in close proximity creates very strong bonds.

Playing games in the same space allows people to fulfil their desire for community, and in this case the game is not so much a window into a different reality as it is an extension of reality.

Online games

Whereas local co-op has the advantage of physical presence, online has the advantage of coverage. When the internet started gaining popularity, people used it to cast their net wider and reach all corners of the world to find community. Online gaming is marvellous, especially for this ability to connect people who would otherwise not have met at all due to where they happen to be located. Something else online is very good at is convenience; it is a lot easier to log in for a couple of hours on a busy work/ school night to play a couple of matches of your favourite multiplayer shooter. Being able to access the game from the comfort of one's home means players can be more spontaneous when deciding to play together since joining a friend online is pretty frictionless. This also usually results in more consistent multiplayer sessions; people find it a lot easier to make plans and stick by them when the location is not an issue.

Although people might technically "prefer" the bond that in-person interaction creates, virtual interaction becomes a preferable alternative, especially when one seems a lot more difficult to achieve than the other. Tools for making presence and communication easier while online gaming have become more and more sophisticated and after the 2020 pandemic, hanging out online has become a lot more common to society at large. The main difference, however, between online and in-person communication is the ability of one person to control more in detail what they show others. Players might choose to keep their video turned off or frame themselves in a specific way, or they might choose to use a microphone or communicate in text. Even if the parties choose to communicate through all the channels possible, not being in the same space means that there is an interpretation gap between the participants. It follows logically that if players spend more time trying to accurately interpret the other's feelings and reactions, there will be less mental space for other playful behaviours around gaming such as the ones occurring during in-person play.

While the difficulty of online communication comes from this interpretation gap, I believe it is also a matter of habit and social skill. In-person communication is what people have done since the dawn of the human race, and with time we have evolved ways of understanding each other's emotions through facial expressions, body language, voice inflections and maybe even, though unknown to us, chemical signals. By comparison, instant long-distance communication has only been around for what feels like a split second in the grand scheme of things.

I believe it is partially about getting used to communicating in this way and partly about creating additional forms of communication in order to fill in those gaps quickly. It takes getting used to because, for the moment, online communication means we cannot use all of the usual senses we use when being in an in-person social situation, only the audio and the visual. Additionally, delays due to lag or other technical limitations such as clarity of picture can break the flow of conversation and break the "illusion" of the other person being with you in the same space at the same time. Some of these aspects will probably improve in the future with new technology, and some of them will be easier for us to accept because it's an expected phenomenon in this type of communication. We can already see this happening in our society now. As a result of the 2020 lockdown, many people have continued communicating online more often because it is something we all got used to doing. Even though we are now free to go out whenever we want and meet with our friends, meeting online is seen as almost just as valuable and in many cases easier to achieve.

Creating ways of more efficiently communicating happens all the time as well. This is why people who spend a lot of time with each other tend to be "in sync". In reality this is our way of adapting to another person's nonverbal cues and deriving more context from something than it is verbally implied. Literature suggests that we derive more than 65% of meaning from non-verbal communication cues when having a real-life conversation (Kumari and Gangwar, 2018), however, it is interesting to discuss how in the context of an online conversation that proportion might change because of all of these barriers and what other avenues people have created to facilitate that online communication.

A great example of this happening at a large scale online is the use of emoji (here used colloquially as a catchall term to mean both emoji and emoticons). Messaging via text can be a little devoid of nuance sometimes, unless of course we spent a lot of time overexplaining everything. But things like sarcasm for example derive from a juxtaposition of content, tone and facial expression that once explained loses its purpose. There is also another reason why users might find the need for an additional tool to express emotion: expedience. Unlike sending a letter, sending and receiving a text message happens virtually instantaneously, therefore it is understood that the purpose of this form of communication is about quickly and efficiently trying to convey the answer we are trying to put forward much like a real conversation. If we are having a conversation in person, for example, we cannot spend too much time thinking about how to express ourselves. This is why humans over time have evolved communication devices that make us more efficient. Emoji therefore have been born from this double need for efficiency and subtlety, and understanding how to use them became the language of the internet. Like other communication devices, emoji evolve in style and meaning as time goes by. Although initially emoji were used in a very literal way (i.e. I am happy so I will send a smiling emoji), with time they became abstracted from their initial pictorial meaning and started being used in a non-literal sense (i.e. I am unhappy or annoyed so I will use the smiling emoji insincerely) (Figure 3.1).

Similar to using emoji when communicating online, a lot of online games make additional communication devices for the players to use during gameplay in order to make communication more efficient and more nuanced. Here are the communication devices most commonly used: pings, emotes and inter-avatar interaction. While these are not limited to games that are played online only, they are put in place mostly to mitigate the downsides of not having full direct communication with the other player

Pings are the online video game equivalent of pointing at something in order to add context to something the person has already communicated. Some games opt for a more complex ping system that gives the other players context about what you are trying to communicate, not only what you are "pointing" at. This is a functional communication device; it ensures players can cooperate and quickly give each other information about the game world. This is predominantly to help with ludus and the

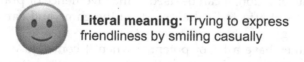
Literal meaning: Trying to express friendliness by smiling casually

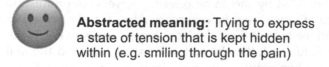
Abstracted meaning: Trying to express a state of tension that is kept hidden within (e.g. smiling through the pain)

Figure 3.1 Example of emoji literal and abstract meaning

need to solve problems together under the set of rules and the environment the game is offering.

Emotes are oftentimes less practical in nature. Although they could be used to signal the other players and give them more information about something (e.g. using a wave emote to incite other players to come where you are), they are more commonly used for non-strategic communication. Emotes are basically an established communication device that is meant to allow players emotional interaction in the virtual space, like in the earlier example when we talked about players crouching on top of a fallen enemy to show disrespect. Unlike teabagging, which is a subversion of the non-purpose-made crouch to communicate emotion, emotes are designed to express a certain mood rather than being designed for gameplay purposes. This does not mean, however, that players will not use them in unexpected or ironic ways (think back to the smiling emoji example); the more we are used to a communication device, the more we add abstraction layers to the meaning of it. Emotes encourage paidia as they are not necessary to the gameplay but instead are playful behaviours that are meant to engage the imagination.

Inter-avatar interaction is somewhat in between the functional and the emotive. It refers to the non-gameplay related ways of one player engaging with another in the game world (e.g. being able to walk up to a player and shake hands). Interaction with another person's avatar is meant to solidify the feeling of being in the same place at the same time, even if the place is virtual. If we think back to the conversation about identity and how players identify with their avatars, two players' avatars interacting with each other is perceived by the player as them interacting with each other even if there is no physical contact to speak of. Inter-avatar interaction is meant to engage players in paidia, but because of the nature of interaction between avatars, this can have a gameplay ramification as well. Say for example you are playing an online game where you can walk up to another player and give them a hug, temporarily preventing them from moving. Although the intention of this action is to communicate emotion, it can be used to inconvenience or prank other players, meaning it affects the ludus side of the game and can become part of the strategy.

Online games have a lot of potential when it comes to connecting people more frequently and allowing them to engage at a distance with a wider variety of people. Still, the feeling of connection and social bonding needs to be aided by the game offering players communication devices that would otherwise not be necessary when the players are in the same room. With the help of these devices, the problem-solving imposed on the player by ludus and, the ability to fill in the gaps and the make-believe that occurs when paidia is in play, the experience created can be just as fulfilling socially as an in-person experience.

Social play in non-multiplayer games

Watching someone play a video game is not a multiplayer experience, but it is still a very strong social experience. This type of social activity extends beyond the immediate friend circle as well with people forming communities around watching people play video games on Twitch or YouTube. The appeal of watching someone else play a video game while you socialise is simple: it allows us to still have the common experience of the game while at different levels of personal involvement. Playing video games is a recreational activity, but it takes both skill and effort to engage with it, an effort that the people watching might not want to invest at that point in time. People might also have different levels of ability both in comprehending the game and in executing the actions needed by the game. This is why many games can foster social play while not being strictly multiplayer, and having varying levels of input as far as the gaming is concerned does not invalidate the fact that it was a social movement formed around the act of play.

There are different types of social play in non-multiplayer games and we can categorise them based on how much active contribution the different parties have:

- Taking turns
- Copilot gaming
- Streaming
- Audience participation

Taking turns

Taking turns is a common experience for a lot of people, especially in childhood. When we are thinking about engaging in social play (even if that play is done with toys), there is a common understanding that in order to successfully play with others we must share. We will not be going into details on the ethics of compelling children to share the objects of play in order to encourage them to become part of a social circle even when they don't want to, as it extends beyond the purpose of this book. But the social value in sharing our belongings with others is indisputable and if done willingly it becomes a way for individuals to bond over a common experience.

Taking turns to play the same single-player video game can be a very cooperative experience even if the players are not engaging with the game at the same time in a traditional multiplayer fashion. Players may decide when and how they take turns playing the game with in-house rules, and these rules are meant to accommodate a specific desired social interaction. Say for example that three siblings are "playing the same game". Two are watching and the third one is playing; they are patiently waiting for their turn and they all want to engage with the game equally. In this case, getting your turn is a reward. To make it equitable they might decide that it is "fair" to switch after a certain amount of time has passed or they might decide to do it based on skill (e.g. when one fails they must pass the controller to the next person).

This is only one of the scenarios possible, but as mentioned before, depending on the goal of the social interaction, sharing control of the game could play out completely differently. Let's consider another scenario. Say I am trying to convince my young relative that games are cool, but they don't have the motor skills to play games that require a lot of precision. When playing together they are playing most of the game, but I occasionally take a turn to help out with the parts that require finer motor skills to help them get unstuck and allow them to enjoy the game more. In this case, the turn-taking is not divided equally; in fact I am just a spectator for most of it unless my relative needs my help. The social goal here is not so much to share the same game, instead I am trying to share my love of games with another person and ensure they have the best experience possible.

Some games took this format of social play and made it part of the intended experience. The *Dark Pictures Anthology* games offer a mode called "movie night" where each player claims a character or characters at the beginning of the game and the game prompts the players to pass the controller around when it's that character's turn to be the protagonist. It's debatable if this style of play alone makes the game multiplayer or not, but irrespective of that the structure of the game is there to support a natural behaviour that the developers already noticed in their previous title *Until Dawn*.

Copilot gaming

One of my fondest memories of my childhood is watching my older brother play all kinds of games. In many ways I attribute my current job as a video game designer to him and the good times we shared during summer break when he would play on our family computer and I would sit behind him cheering him on. The circumstances were such for us at the time that we rarely had an opportunity to play together at the same time. Technology was different and we only had a family computer and we didn't have access to consoles that would allow us to play together. But for the two of us, gaming was still highly social, it was the bonding activity we used to do every chance we got. Because I was much younger than he was, I knew a lot less about video games and I could not speak any English. My understanding and interaction with the game was done through him as a conduit. As we grew older the roles kinda swapped with my brother showing me games that he already played, and because I could now understand them and play them properly, he would watch me play to see my reaction to the games he loved.

"Backseat gaming" is often used to indicate the action of comment-ing excessively on the right way to play while not being the one playing, derived from the term "backseat driver". The term has negative connota-tions, implying the input of the person who is not playing is undesirable and bothersome. Because of this I feel like the term does not fit the kind of gaming experience my brother and I had; instead I call it copilot gaming. This is because, much like a copilot, both you and the person "driving" the action in the game are engaging with the game, be it directly or indirectly. In copilot gaming it's not about telling the player what to do while not being the one actually engaging with the game; it's about communication and collaboration around the subject of the game.

"Copilot mode" is also a name used by Xbox for its feature that allows users to use the input of two controllers as a single controller. This is seen as an accessibility feature and less a social feature. It is intended to be used to allow someone with less motor ability to still get involved in play while another person is there to help them out. Although this is a great option to include and it explores similar territory, copilot gaming as defined here does not refer to this type of play. Copilot gaming is also not about silently spectating as if you were watching a movie, because for this to be a social experience between player and non-player(s) communication must occur, and in this case communication about the content of the game.

There are many social reasons why someone would engage with this type of social play. A big one is ability, which we touched upon in my previous example. In this scenario the person playing will act as a way for the person not playing to experience the world of the game, maybe even listening to their instructions and performing them. Watching someone play can also be about the delight of sharing a game with someone, incit-ing them to try a game that you have already experienced in order to see their reaction. In this case the comments are there to guide and encourage. The third and final type is the joint discovery: players might sit down to experience a game together potentially for the first time. In this case the conversation is about what people anticipate should happen next and the decisions are a mix of the player's own opinions as well as the opinions of those watching and commenting. In any of these situations the person controlling the game has technically absolute power of decision, but they choose to share that power with others watching in order to engage with them socially.

Streaming

Watching other people stream games fulfils a similar but slightly differ-ent social need as watching someone we know more closely play a game. However, when engaging with streaming there are two types of social relationships that are at play that viewers might choose to engage with:

forming a sense of community with the other people watching and forming a parasocial relationship with the person streaming.

In general, people are looking for a sense of belonging, and they might choose to interact with others more or less based on their ability and comfort levels in order to achieve said sense of belonging. As the viewer comes into the chat they might keep to themselves or engage with the chat more or less, but part of the appeal of spectating is being there to see how the community reacts to something, not just yourself. Let's give an example outside of video games. First, to make it easier to envision, let's say you decide to go watch your favourite football team in person. You might choose to wear your team's colours, you might interact with other supporters during the match or you might keep the comments and wins to yourself. Even if you choose not to engage in any other way with the community, the act of being in that space places you in a social situation. There is no denying that part of the experience of being in the tribune of a football match is as much about the game being played on the field as it is about the atmosphere and excitement of the fans. Similarly, when watching someone play games on Twitch we are there not only to watch the game but to observe the reaction and interaction between the streamer and their audience as well as between different members of the audience. Even if you choose to not engage with the chat yourself, comments from others keep scrolling in the chat, and the person streaming will likely acknowledge people and hold a conversation (in order to maintain their relationship with the audience). Whatever happens in the game and on the screen is influenced by the presence of the audience, their comments and the fact that the purpose of streaming is for people to consume it as entertainment. We could argue that it is not the game itself that is the centre point of the social interaction but rather the performance of play. This is interesting because going back to ludus and paidia, the streamer playing the game is engaging with ludus in order to "win" the game (whatever the win condition is in the case). The audience on the other hand is not engaged in play directly, but they engage with the streamer in the joint imagination of what that game is about. So while this is technically not paidia on the viewer's part, they are witnessing the paidia like space of the person playing and interpreting what it happening while also "performing" as a streamer.

Let's go back to the children's play example in order to draw some parallels and understand this phenomenon better. Let's say two children are playing doctor, and an adult is watching them play. The adult is not part of the paidia play that the children are engaging with, but they can bear witness to that imagination space by observing them play, and listening to what they say to each other and even the explanations that the children may give directly to the adult. In the same way, the audience is not technically part of the play, they feel like they are because of sharing this imagination space with the person actively controlling the game.

Another reason why streaming works so well is the formation of a parasocial relationship (Ballantine and Martin, 2005) between the streamer and their audience. This term defines a performer's relationship with their audience in which the people watching get a sense of personally knowing the creator they are following by consuming the content they create. This is particularly relevant when talking about online spaces where the content is specifically designed in a way to suggest this is the performer's "true self" (i.e. streaming, product reviews, opinion pieces, etc.) rather than performing a role (i.e. acting as a character in a skit or a show). To what degree this relationship is real or a illusion of a connection is debatable and differs on a case-by-case basis. However, what we need to keep in mind for the purposes of this book is that there is a relationship that forms over time be it "real" or "perceived". While watching a streamer's content, the audience grows closer to that person over time and the interaction becomes more similar to watching a friend play a game. Feeding into that feeling of familiarity to the user is also in the streamer's interest as engaged viewers might make donations or convince their friends to also watch the stream. From the streamer's side, the more successful they are at appearing familiar to the audience and having their audience grow, the more difficult it becomes for them to connect to each individual and instead see them as more of a collective. This is where parasocial relationships truly differ from regular social relationships: the audience has permanent access to the streamer as an individual, while on the other side, if the streamer is successful, they have less and less access to the audience members as individuals. This however does not mean that these relationships are less valuable for people who want to engage with them or that they are established in bad faith by the streamers solely for financial benefit, it just means that the perceived degree of closeness will differ on the two sides of the relationship.

Audience play

Audience play is there to create a sense of equal ownership over the game experience. This implies that the community takes control of the actual game in some way (Twitch Plays *Pokémon*) where the game input is crowdsourced. Unlike streaming where the audience participation happens through the medium of one person controlling the game while occasionally communicating or consulting with the people, audience play is more direct and allows everyone to become the player.

Audience play is quite commonly used in game shows, where people get to play along with the competitors on screen or have a special section dedicated to audience interaction. Audience play is in this situation meant to give the players a way to relate to the content happening on the TV screen, because unlike a streamer who is communicating with their audience, game shows follow a tighter script and therefore need to insert specific times in the "script" to involve their audience. In situations like this, audience play can take multiple forms:

- **Audience competition**: There is something for people to win if they participate (e.g. be the first to call us with the right answer and win a prize)
- **Audience decisions**: People have a part to play in the decisions made usually via a voting mechanism
- **Follow-along**: People play the game at the same time as it is played on screen (this can be self-enforced meaning players do on their own for fun or there could be a way of interacting with an automated system that receives answers online or other means of communication such as messaging)

But audience play is not reserved for game shows. As mentioned before, there have been other ways this kind of play has been attempted. Twitch plays come to mind as a particular example, but also games that function like a TV show where the "participants" are also the audience like the trivia game *HQ*.

This is definitely a more experimental and underserved area of social play, but there is a lot of work being done especially around streaming platforms such as Twitch, and I believe there is plenty of interest for this to be explored further in the near future. We could argue that audience play is a newer type of multiplayer that is designed for large numbers of people and in some way it is. If multiplayer is about joint input into the same game this will definitely fit that criteria. But different types of audience play behave differently, with some not offering players direct control and some designing an auxiliary part of the game to be played only by the audience, so defining it as pure multiplayer did not seem to fit it in its current form.

Part 2

The beginnings of social gaming

chapter 4

The birth of social media gaming

Social media started out a lot differently than we might think of it today, and it's difficult to put in perspective exactly how much the platforms have changed in what is ultimately a pretty short time. In the very early days of social media the focus was predominantly on creating a profile that represented you, much like curating your own web page. People could go to your MySpace page and get to know more about you, what music you liked, see pictures you uploaded and your overall aesthetic. In short, social media was not focusing on the social exchange between people but on creating a social profile. When Facebook entered the social media scene it was much like its predecessors, but with time the interest of Facebook shifted from creating an online representation to "keeping up" with your connections. This was a fundamental moment because it opened the door for social media to be something users check periodically to see what the people they knew were up to. And this is also when games started to make more sense for the platform. Texas hold 'em poker (*Zynga Poker*) made by Zynga was the first game to appear on Facebook in 2007; this was a pretty shy start to what would be Facebook gaming. But while we will go on to talk in more detail about the journey of Facebook and how it shaped the way we think about games on a social platform, it's worth noting that it was not the first to experiment with "social gaming" as a concept in a space where people were already "gathering" online.

Messengers and the precursors of social games

From the late 1990s to the mid-2000s messenger apps were very popular, with programs like MSN Messenger or Yahoo! Messenger becoming the way to stay in touch with friends online aside from email. Both MSN and Yahoo! Messenger were offering an array of games to their users, some of which were more akin to apps or playful experiences. None of the games on these platforms rose to the sort of popularity that games on Facebook ended up at, but they no doubt opened a door for developers to think about what kind of experiences users can share in a social context online.

Yahoo! Messenger had a pretty varied array of games that were incarnations of games from other platforms, instead of being purpose-designed with the qualities and the quirks of the platform explicitly in mind. The main purpose of these games was not to explore the possibility of social

DOI: 10.1201/9781003314325-6

interaction between the users but rather to entertain the novelty of being able to play a game in such a space. Similarly, MSN had an array of applications and games that users could engage with, most of them adaptations of games that came with Windows like Minesweeper or Solitaire.

It is a natural progression for new platforms to experiment with porting already existing experiences in order to test the boundaries of user interactions and the tech itself before testing the boundaries of design on those platforms. If we are to look back to the very first game ever made, *Pong* was nothing but a video representation of table tennis. Following the same line of thinking, the games and apps on messengers were there to test the waters and see how interested people would be in playing games in that setting. This was the first step on the path of social gaming as it showed there was an opportunity to add game platforms where people gather in order to increase engagement. Furthermore, it showed that when porting a social experience from physical to digital or even from one platform to another, adjustments would have to be made for the game to offer a quality social experience.

Messenger programs like MSN Messenger and Yahoo! Messenger eventually got taken over by other means of communication that were more immediate, and with them the very incipient form of what we would later call social games got shut down, but the opportunity of using messenger apps as a home for entertainment is still explored today by different platforms. In later chapters I will be delving deeper into my journey with social games on the different messaging apps and how that shaped my opinion on what a social game is. But before we move on to a more recent time, it is important to start with the explosion of social games and the journey of games on Facebook.

Facebook gaming

As mentioned earlier, Facebook gaming started similarly to the messenger games of the early 2000s. A version of poker, an already well-known and hugely popular social card game, was published for the platform by Zynga to test the waters in 2007. The intention was to explore the landscape of this new platform that was Facebook gaming and get a sense of the overall appetite of the audience for that sort of experience.

In 2008 when Facebook's growth really started to accelerate, Big Viking Games put out *YoVille*, which was then later also sold to Zynga. The game is described as a virtual world that has a very different vibe from the poker game that was launched a year prior. It was a lot closer to other life sim games like *The Sims*, but instead of the player taking the role of a god looking over digital characters, the players were encouraged to create a single avatar that was meant to represent themselves in the YoWorld. The game offered players the ability to role-play and socialise in the virtual space, which at the time had only really been done in larger massively multiplayer online role-playing games (MMORPGs) or virtual worlds like *Second Life*. The difference between *YoVille* and something like *Second Life* was how accessible it was to the public and that this was all happening in an environment where other people you knew were also "hanging out". This is why the game was not presented so much as a game but as a virtual space to be in with others you knew, which is very similar to the more modern concept of the "Metaverse".

The game became very popular on the platform, with public sources citing their daily active users reaching over 5 million within their first year of the game being live. These numbers are incredible even compared to the most popular MMOs and yet many people might have never heard of *YoVille* and the impact it had on the games industry. These games have managed to tap into a market we call today "casual gamers", who were at the time not really considered to be "into games" when in reality the right games had not yet been made for them. While Facebook games were managing for the first time to captivate this audience sector, a very nascent App Store was also setting its eyes on a similar market that would end up playing a part in the later decline of Facebook games as they used to be.

In 2009 *FarmVille* was released and it took the world of Facebook by storm reaching 20 million users by October of the same year. *FarmVille* was not however the first title of its type on the platform: the earlier-released *Farm Town* was a near replica of the game and some would argue it should have been the one to explode. The popularity of *FarmVille* boiled down to two simple things: user acquisition and A/B testing of social mechanics. Lessons from the previous games it had published (both *Zynga Poker* and *YoVille*) pointed Zynga to the importance of social interaction and notifications. While the tactic of it can be considered aggressive, *FarmVille* got to be so popular because it was taking into consideration the existing behaviour of the audience and Zynga had the means and the wherewithal to use it to its advantage.

In order to better understand what that means, we need to look more closely at a couple of specific mechanics that *FarmVille* used in order to engage the Facebook audience:

- Social interaction as a substitute for financial investment
- Gifting and trading
- Appointment mechanics

Social points in exchange for time and money

FarmVille came out as a free-to-play (F2P) game in a time when there were not a whole lot of them. We have to remember that even though the concept is incredibly well understood today and used in many different ways across the games industry, this was not the case back in 2009. The game primarily relied on microtransactions to make its money, as monetisation strategies for the F2P were also still in their infancy. But unlike other non-social contemporaries, *FarmVille* had another kind of "currency" that it could shift that I like to call "social points".

It is no surprise that when making any kind of social multiplayer game, the design should be such that the experience of playing with others is a better experience than playing alone. The most common ways to do this are presence related and surface level. To give an example, being able to "visit" the farm of your friend enforces a feeling of connection and makes the game more "fun" to play with friends rather than strangers or even alone. These sorts of mechanics are valuable in creating a good social experience. But the "good time" someone is having with a social play situation versus a single-player situation is incredibly difficult to quantify for the players and it's difficult to control or keep track of for the developers. These mechanics will have a different effect depending on who we are addressing; some players would enjoy doing it for the sake of the interaction but for others, the reward of "fun" will not be sufficient.

There is also another facet of such mechanics, which is that players will not get to truly experience this unless they already went over the hump of inviting a friend in the first place. Sure the game can attempt to explain such social mechanics by involving other players or by creating a fake scenario, but the feeling of actually connecting with someone you know in a game is emotionally very different and it cannot be faked. This is why features such as these are additive; they are great to have on top of everything else, but they cannot be the main and only motivation for the player to invite someone.

In order to make the player understand the benefits of having a friend join them, the incentive to invite them has to be very clear. This can be done fundamentally in one of two ways:

- Restricted content, which encourages the player's curiosity and, to a degree, fear of missing out. This means that some parts of the game will be entirely inaccessible to the player unless they are playing with someone else.
- Helping hand, which relies on the player wanting to bypass or speed up parts of the game, which can only be achieved with someone else's help.

Although the wrapping is different for the two methods the outcome is fundamentally the same: the goal is to make the player understand that with the addition of a friend they are going to have a better time playing the game.

Restricting content for a specific number of players is a bit of a danger-ous technique, although it can prove very effective if the players are already involved with the game. The reason why this works for engaged players and not for new ones is perceived value. When asking someone they know to play a game with them, the player uses social points in order to convince their friend to join. Therefore, the "item" they are trying to obtain in the game by inviting said person has to be of greater or equal value in order for them to do it. For an engaged player, the value is obvious, they enjoy the game and want more of the same content; but for a new player who doesn't know yet if they like the game, the exchange is not yet worth it.

The helping hand method is a lot simpler and a lot more accessible for new players. The core idea is to allow the players to do everything completely by themselves but show to them the usefulness of getting help from a friend to complete tasks that would otherwise take longer or be more difficult. In this case, the value the player placed upon this task is a lot clearer because it's derived from two real-world components: time and money. The value of a task being completed is equivalent to how much time and/or money the player would have otherwise invested for that task to be done. This is still linked to how much the player cares about the game, after all, if they don't care about it why would they bother "fin-ishing" a task? But giving real-life value to digital events does enforce a certain kind of "exchange rate". Furthermore, in these F2P games, time is money, as the games use the slowing of progresses as an incentive for the player to spend real-life money.

Allowing the player to exchange social points to circumvent the game's monetisation could be seen as counterintuitive initially, especially for a business whose aim is to make a profit from an F2P game, but it is actually a very clever strategy. It relies on multiple layers of F2P monetisa-tion philosophy and here is how it works.

The percentage of players who engage with in-app purchases is very low. The percentage varies from game to game, but overall it's safe to say that a mean value would be 1%–2%. Given this breakdown, it's a lot easier to understand this strategy. If a player does not want to spend their money in the game, the best thing they can do to help the game's monetisation is to help the game reach more people in hopes that one of those people will be willing to spend money.

Figure 4.1 describes a possible scenario. For every person invited to the game, there are three options possible:

- They can use social points to progress and incentivise others to play.
- They can engage with the monetisation in order to avoid spending social points.
- They can stop playing.

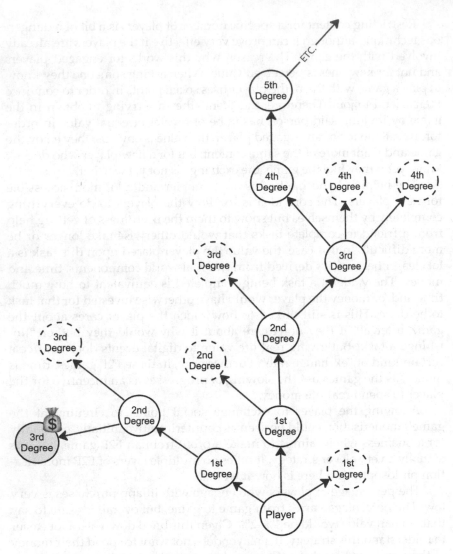

Figure 4.1 Social graph showing how player invites can be used to boost monetisation

For this structure to work, however, the game balancing has to slow down past a certain point in order to "force" the player to be reliant on either of the two methods of progressing. But there is ultimately one major flaw in this system and it has to do with saturation. In the beginning when a game is expanding, it is a lot easier to find people who have not interacted with the game and try to convince them to join. Past a certain point, however, when everyone on Facebook seemed to be playing *FarmVille*, it was impossible to escape notifications and posts about it. People were being spammed from all directions with game-related notifications. This meant that not only did recipients start ignoring them, but it also meant that now it was increasingly frowned upon to send such notifications, therefore the cost in social points had increased due to saturation.[1]

This very strategy is what brought *FarmVille* to the heights of its popularity but it was also what ultimately sparked the most criticism of it. While some of the talk about the game was elitist and unfounded and had more to do with what was worth calling "a real game", some of the criticism about the game's "spammy" nature raised real issues to do with the structure of its social monetisation strategy and how it affected the social media space. In the end, the ideas explored in games like FarmVille will take different forms over time, and platforms will also move towards having stricter rules regarding the frequency of notifications and informed consent regarding the content being shared. But another side of this story belongs to the users and how their understanding of the online space has changed their opinions on such mechanics. In the next chapter, I will go into more detail about how users and platforms changed the landscape of games on Facebook.

Gifting, trading and asynchronous multiplayer

The idea for gifting or trading in video games was not new when *FarmVille* was made; many games had done it before in their own way and even the predecessor *YoVille* experimented with this mechanic. But gifting and trading would become one of the most powerful social media game tools over the years. To understand why this is such a powerful mechanic we'll have to discuss in a little more detail the Facebook climate at the time and the audience appetite for multiplayer.

It might be easy to forget nowadays that Facebook started as a desktop application. In fact, when these games were coming out in 2009 there were barely any apps to speak of, smartphones were not accessible to everyone and neither was 24/7 access to the internet. It is truly incredible to think of exactly how much has changed in the last 14 years and how access to both the internet and powerful smartphones has shaped the way we think of social media, creating a completely different climate for communication and games on the platforms. Given that Facebook was thought of as predominantly a desktop application, all of these games while "casual" were not "portable" in the same way that mobile games are nowadays, so they were not designed to fill the same niche. Instead of what games like *FarmVille* and *YoVille* were experimenting with in trying to use games in order to engage with others, the casual nature of these games came as a result of designing for a wide audience, a digital case of convergent evolution if you will.

Given both the lack of portability and the casual nature of the audience, *FarmVille* could not be a very involved synchronous "multi-player" game even though the focus was to bring people together. For this very reason, asynchronous multiplayer features were fundamental to getting across the idea that these games were meant to be a social experience. I will discuss asynchronous and synchronous multiplayer in more detail in later chapters, but for the moment all we need to truly understand is that there is no superior type of multiplayer and they are not orthogonal to each other either. Of course they build different experiences for the players, but ultimately the choice of using sync or async lies in the kind of habits that players exhibit around the game. Let's imagine for a moment that *FarmVille* was not as it was and instead it was a continuous world with sync multiplayer features where players could only interact with their friends when they were all online at the same time. While it might sound compelling to your general game audience, this would have not been a good fit for the casual audience at the time. Say for example that the user logged into Facebook every day twice a day when they had access to a computer with internet on it. They had limited time to spend on the platform, as they had other things to attend to; managing to actually coordinate with someone they knew to play at the same time would have required a lot more effort and the likelihood of the schedules not matching was way too high. So making the game synchronous would have actually made the social mechanic of the game inaccessible to a lot of the players and reduced the feeling of a joint experience.

While async initially sounds like it does not allow for the same kind of connection that seeing your friend in the game in real time does, the light-touch nature of it makes it easy to access for people who would like to engage with their friends but can't because of how incredibly difficult scheduling such things can be. Gifting and trading are great async mechanics. They allow the player to establish a connection with someone they know without the other person being with them in the game at the same time. Furthermore, the exchange of virtual objects means that players might return to the game to receive something from a friend, which is a good incentive to come back and a great feeling to give the player.

Nowadays we have a lot more levers to pull in order to create a great social multiplayer experience, but all of those things are afforded to us by the advancement in technology. In 2009's social media climate, the methods they used to give players a sense of connection with their friends were well informed by how people were using the platform at the time. This exploration of how to make people connect in a game without actually seeing each other in the virtual world laid out the groundwork for a lot of features that mobile games would adopt and use to great success over time.

In future chapters I will go into more detail about how very similar systems and mechanics are used in today's climate to aid in making a fulfilling social gaming experience.

Making players leave so they come back later

The word "immersion" is everywhere in game literature, and many games strive to achieve it to some degree. After all, we want the player to suspend their disbelief in order to create great experiences and memories. But as discussed in a previous chapter, games and playful behaviour are more of a spectrum than we sometimes give it credit for. When we engage with a game, what mixture of ludus and paidia are at play is determined not only by the game structures but also by the willingness and ability of the players to engage with the ruleset and the fantasy of the game. Over the years, I have seen a lot of people, developers, players and writers question the value of casual games because they focus less on immersion and more on tactile fun and quick rewards. But given what we discussed earlier in this chapter, what happens if the audience does not want and need to get immersed in order to enjoy the game for its other playful features? After all, if a game is objectively immersive but nobody plays it, it ultimately ends up doing a poor job of immersing anyone.

The reason why I wanted to mention it in this chapter is because I believe immersion and time are two components of the same equation, and they have to be treated as such. When we talk about time we are really referring to two things: the time that the player is happy to spend in any one independent game session and how much time it would take the game to engage the player in the world. These two aspects are intrinsically linked to one another; if the player's ability and desire to spend time in the game is shorter than the time the game needs in order to immerse them into the world, then the fantasy of the game cannot be established for the player and the attempt fails. This is a problem a lot of casual games need to solve one way or another, and because a casual audience has in theory less time and desire to engage in long uninterrupted sessions of gameplay, the game has to accommodate them. But how exactly do they do that? The answer is using appointment mechanics to control session length and frequency.

In 2009 when *FarmVille* was first coming out, the concept of using certain mechanics to actively deter the player from playing long sessions sounded a bit like madness. The point with most other games that had been made previously was that the only way to engage the player was to keep them in the game session as long as possible. While this still applies to some games, it is not the only way to do things. The concept around curbing the amount of things players can do in any given session is actually very simple and it works in multiple ways with the format that *FarmVille* had:

1. Give the players a quick intro, get them to enjoy the game and make them feel like they have "earned" something by playing
2. Pinpoint the moment at which causal players would naturally want to quit the session and give them something to do that can happen while they are away (e.g. plant crops that take longer than a single session to grow)
3. Notify the player that the timer has completed in order to incentivise them to return

This is a very simple and well-known structure nowadays and it's still being used to great effect. Apart from its obvious advantage of encouraging the player to rejoin the game, there are other side effects to time mechanics that are also beneficial. Firstly, it supports the monetisation of the free-to-play game; players could purchase fertiliser in order to speed up the timer. But another, potentially less obvious benefit was to the social aspects of the game, making sure the player returns to the game periodically meant they were more likely to see and interact with requests from neighbours, which would in turn remind those neighbours to return.

Apart from appointment mechanics, timing is also extremely important when it comes to gratification for the player, and this is another expectation that differs between casual and hardcore players. When opening a game the expectation of most players is that the game will in some way satisfy their need for entertainment. Each player has a different expectation for the kind of satisfaction they are looking for and how long they are happy to wait until it is given to them. You might have heard about this concept in shooter games where it's being called "time to shotgun". All games have a version of this concept, but the object of gratification is different. The "shotgun" represents how much time the player should invest in a game before they can "really start having fun". It's important to remember the mechanical aspect of the proverbial "shotgun" because this is not only about prizes, it is specifically about rewarding mechanisms within the game that enforce the main loop and encourage the player to keep engaging with the systems and play more.

In *FarmVille*, gratification is done quite simply and effectively, and players are given crops already ready to harvest as soon as they start the game. This might be misinterpreted as giving away the "prize" too early; after all, the perceived value of something that took no effort to achieve is not very high. However, the most exciting thing about the game is not really harvesting, it's selling. Selling the crops feels good because the player had to put some effort into harvesting and they now have empty plots they can plant new crops on; this is how the loop is being enforced. Also, in the very first set of crops, the player gets a plant "in progress", which will only be ready to harvest after a certain amount of time. This showcases the appointment mechanic, and because the player already harvested some of the same crops they have an understanding of the value the items have versus the time it takes to grow them.

All in all, time-based mechanics have more to do with the casual nature of these games than it has to do with the social nature, but it's easy to see that making the game as casual and accessible as possible allowed people to convince a lot of their friends to play. Without their casual nature, these games would not have been able to make their way into so many people's routines for such a long time, and the appointment mechanics made sure people got reminded every day of the game they had "running" in the background.

Many of the mechanics discussed here will go on to be refined in time and incorporated into the roster of standard features for a casual free-to-play game, and we will go deeper into how they have been refined and how they are being used today in the following chapters.

I believe it is worth mentioning that apart from big players like Zynga, other games and companies were looking to fill the same gap in the market, and they all contributed in some way to the phenomenon that social games ended up being. It is quite unfortunate that the reality of such new markets is that those who discover and explore a niche first are likely not the ones known by history for having brought something to the public. When we look at the history of what came to be, being as recent as this, we have to remember that oftentimes there are more complex factors at play than a simple "who's idea was this really". It is all about good timing, financial investment and, last but not least, "refinement" of an idea. Most of these mechanical ideas worked when they got refined and used in a specific context and it is a lot easier to explore these topics through the lens of popular games such as *FarmVille*. That does not however diminish the contribution of the other games and people who worked on uncovering these methods in the first place, but it is a testament to the "right place at the right time" nature of its growth.

In the next chapter I will go over the circumstances and the reasons that I believe were the biggest contributors to the decline in popularity of Facebook games after the initial boom and incredible popularity in the very early 2010s.

Note

1. See here an animated diagram that shows the flow of invites and the spread of invites: https://my.machinations.io/d/social-spread/56412cb78dd811eebb 1902473fb09e27.

chapter 5

The fall of Facebook social games

As the mid-2010s were approaching, Facebook games were still going strong and there was still a huge influx of new users onto the platform, which meant that even if some people got sick and tired of the avalanche of notifications that was slowly inundating everyone's Facebook walls, there were still many new users who were willing to try it. The spammy nature of these games was often cited as a main source of frustration for many of the users be they gamers or non-gamers. The reality is that, however irritating, the notifications worked and kept bringing people in so there was no real incentive to change it. And while notification saturation did not help the market, it was not the most significant hurdle for these games, instead it was the shift to mobile that really shook the world of Facebook at large and by extension the games that called that platform their home.

Mobile versions of Facebook existed since 2008 (iOS), but the mobile market was still very young. In 2011, Messenger was published as a standalone mobile app and in 2012, Facebook went native with its apps to improve performance. This series of events was an attempt by the platform to remain relevant in the very quickly shifting tech environment. But during this shift, the games that made waves on the platforms just a few years back were left behind. The early Facebook games were not designed for mobile. There is no way to actually pinpoint the moment in which the decline started; it was more a case of death by a thousand cuts. While companies like Zynga tried to adapt to the particularity of the new platforms with mobile versions and sequels, none reached the heights of the original *FarmVille*.

The downward trajectory was also determined by some very stiff competition in the mobile market. It's worth remembering that as smartphones became popular, the casual game market grew rapidly and several high-quality mobile games became part of people's routines. The convenience of playing games on a device that you could carry with you all the time made casual gamers use their mobile phone as their main source of entertainment. While none of these games had all the same social capabilities and features that Facebook afforded games on its platform, a lot of games started to experiment with linking the user's Facebook account to the game. In this new form, social mechanics will keep being experimented on within the mobile space while Facebook games lay dormant ready to change again.

DOI: 10.1201/9781003314325-7

The internet was changing

The early to mid-2010s marked a significant time in a multitude of ways: people's attitudes towards the internet were changing as rules and regulations were coming into place and as people began to understand more about the ramifications of online life. A lack of tech and internet literacy in the parent generation led to a lot of concern over what children and teenagers were doing online, especially on social media. While the internet was previously all about fabricated personas on forums and people using pseudonyms to write in personal blogs, social media was all about the real identity of people, their real friends, where they lived and where they travelled. This led to a generation of teens that grew up connected all the time, and I was part of it. While the concern about privacy came predominantly out of a desire to protect children on these platforms, it ultimately exposed an issue that was far more widespread than online bullying (even though the dangers of that are not to be minimised). Concerns about keeping data safe started to swell in the mid-2010s, and even though the new General Data Protection Regulation (GDPR) would not come into effect until 2018, the internet users of 2014–2016 were a lot more aware of how data collected from them could be used sometimes in their favour and other times in their detriment.

This was followed by a legislative shift, but another shift that was more important for the world of social games was a change in mentality to do with what people would share on these platforms. The adolescents who would spam their entire Facebook list with *FarmVille* notifications grew up and started to understand the power of content shares. These same people educated their family members about the dangers of online, bringing much-needed internet literacy into the lives of those who were just starting out with the internet be they young children or late adopters.

Beyond the concern for data and privacy, users started to understand the use of social media as a place to cultivate a specific image, create a story for their life and gain praise and recognition from those they were connected with. This also meant that the quality of a share had to be higher than what users were used to. People did not want to post something that would ruin their curated image. In the following chapters we will go into more detail about how sharing has changed in more recent times, especially for Gen Z who are considered to be the first generation to have fully grown up with the internet at their fingertips. But overall it is safe to say that as users became more familiar with social media, they became more conscious and more aware of what was posted on their feeds. It would be incorrect to say that this shift "killed" sharing because while it did make people more aware of what they put on their profiles making it harder to convince them to initiate, the shares themselves became higher quality, which acted like a counter-effect on the notification oversaturation and noisiness that Facebook was experiencing at the height of *FarmVille*.

The mobile environment and Messenger

As a platform, Facebook adapted overall really well when the switch from desktop to mobile happened. Facebook's decision to split their product into the Facebook app and the Messenger app was ultimately beneficial, as it split the two most important aspects of the platform into more manageable apps that people could use independently of each other. But with this shift there was a bit of a question regarding games: where should they live, in the main app or the messenger app? In 2016 Instant Games was launched as an attempt to shift the games on the platform to the messenger app and create a multipurpose platform where people could drop in and instantly play a game with their friends. This was potentially riffing on the older idea for messenger games from the early 2000s. Incidentally, this is where my journey started as a social games designer trying to elucidate the mystery that was this new stage of social games.

The environment of Facebook Instant Games was very different from the desktop games of the early 2010s and the most fundamental difference was the way that they thought about social multiplayer. As previously discussed, games like *FarmVille* relied very heavily on sharing people's Facebook walls. The idea was that shares about *FarmVille* could be encountered "in the wild" on someone else's profile updates, much like an ad or a website banner. There was clear potential for "selling" things to users by implanting ads onto those news feeds and Facebook took the opportunity to advertise to people in this manner. I would not be surprised if this idea was inspired or supported by the success of the game's notifications.

This type of share is called "one-to-many" and the logic behind it is that if the person shares to multiple other people, the likelihood of one of those people being interested and clicking is higher. This is basically a form of "user acquisition" that is led by the existing users. But the shift to mobile and especially the shift to messenger meant the focus of the shares shifted from one-to-many to one-to-one. While it sounds counterintuitive, there are a few reasons why the shift made logical sense:

1. **It aligns better with the purpose of Messenger**: People used the Messenger side of Facebook to communicate directly in pairs or in small groups.
2. **Shares can be more specific**: While one-to-many shares have to be "impersonal" in order to appeal to a wide range of people, one-to-one shares can be personalised and directed making them higher quality.
3. **There are fewer but higher-quality shares**: While the reach is narrower because people send fewer direct shares, the chances of actually getting a response to the share are higher because the social relationship between the sender and responder is stronger and there is more social obligation to respond.

This shift in focus came not only from the change in platform but also from the change in people's perception of shares and how frequently they saw them. The human brain gets very good at ignoring things we see a lot and we consider irrelevant. This is why with time advertisements just seem to disappear into the web page; we know they are there but we don't register what they are about. The "news feed" used to be just that: a series of updates of what your friends have done recently on Facebook. When game shares and adverts worked their way into the timeline, people instinctively started to gloss over them and move on. This is why I suspect the generic one-to-many shares no longer worked after a certain point in time: people just lumped them together with the other advertisements they got served and scrolled by.

But Messenger presented a new opportunity to explore a more intimate kind of play, the sort of multiplayer that was not really even possible on the platform only a few years prior. The centre of interaction was now on the connection between individuals and the mobile format, and the advancement in tech opened the way for a different kind of games design to be explored. In this era of Facebook games a lot of the ideas around what my team and I would later dub "hyper-social games" were explored, and we experimented with many different mechanics to better understand what this new form of play was all about. The next chapters will go into more detail about the kind of experimentation we have done with mechanics and what we learned from it.

It is fair to say that after this change, however, Facebook games as they used to be were no longer. They remained active, but their popularity dwindled and some of them transitioned to mobile in order to make due. The original *FarmVille* stopped being supported by Zynga in 2020 and none of the following titles under the same IP reached the same heights as it did in 2009.

Late adopters and audience change

When looking at player cohorts in who is adopting certain tech and why, for social media especially, early adopters tended to be in their teens or early 20as. Facebook started as a campus-size experiment, but as it grew into a business and started to enter its "early majority stage" (Rogers, 1962) a lot of users were those who were already used to technology and the internet. In general this meant the younger segment of the population (obviously plenty of exceptions existed). This segment of the population was also more familiar with games and therefore more likely to engage with someone inviting them to play. Because of this, the "maximum" popularity of Facebook games could have actually been reached long before the new user numbers ever even started to slow down because the appetite for games was held mostly by the early majority adopters. Obviously, these are generalisations and it's difficult to pinpoint when the new users joining the platform stopped having a directly proportional effect on the game audience, as other factors were at play at the same time. But it's important to note that demographic data should not be ignored when looking at this kind of story because while it's not a good idea to presuppose things about the individual by looking at the age bracket they fit in, averages tell us some things about mass behaviours.

But what do I actually mean by mass behaviours? For example, we know the stage in our life plays an important role in our gaming habits, and while individuals might be in different stages of their lives at different ages, the general trend is that people will start employment in their late teens to early 20s. This impacts a huge component in our ability to enjoy any kind of entertainment not just games, and that component is time. Through the lifetime of Facebook, not only has the late majority increased the age of the average user but the audience itself has aged. This meant that on average they had less time to spend in front of a desktop computer playing a game as work and home responsibilities took over their lives. And the fact that these games were on desktop was crucial here because if we compare this with the demographic of mobile games a new story emerges: it's all about convenience and accessibility. When users could very easily download a mobile game to fill the time on their commute to work, the interest in games expanded to encompass a larger segment of the population than people ever thought possible all because of convenience.

With time, the popularity of Facebook as a platform diminished among the teen and early 20s sector. Partially because of the adoption of other social media more suited to their needs but also partially because of the popularity of the platform with the older generation. Facebook became in the eyes of the Gen Z a place where they communicate with their family or older relatives more so than a place where they spend time with their friends; it was no longer the "cool place to be".[1] In the UK the biggest user segment of Facebook by age in 2022 was 24–34, and the second largest was 35–44,[2] and the stats look quite similar for other prominent tech markets as well. These stats, however, do not reveal how active users are on these platforms and how likely they are to engage with peripheral content on these platforms beyond just keeping up with other people's updates. Data from 2020 suggests that "games" are not even among the top activities for Facebook users.[3] However, Meta's own publicly available statistics suggest that 350 million-plus monthly active users "play instant games" (citing internal data from 2020),[4] so people are still engaging with these games but the visibility of them has changed dramatically.

In 2018 I had the opportunity to explore the scene of instant games and find out what was working and what was not working. Historically we knew from the older generation of social games that wall posts were the most efficient in gathering interest and virally growing. In 2018 the mechanics we were experimenting with were trying to find out what ratio of one-to-one and one-to-many sharing was right for the platform. Something we seemed to find time and time again with hyper-social games is that no matter the platform the one-to-one sharing created very strong responder bonds, where the people coming into the game invited by others tended to really stick around for a long time, the main issue was visibility, and that is what the one-to-many shares were meant to be helping with.

In 2019 a type of instant "game" seemed to be really breaking through to the audience, and that type of game was the personality test type. These games had no gameplay, but they had "personalised" content that could be easily shared to Facebook walls. The simplicity of this seemed to be just the right amount of interaction and the fact that the main sharing mechanism was to make a wall post really caught on to the Facebook market at the time. What followed was an inevitable wave of clones that flooded the market incredibly quickly. And while it's easy to dismiss these types of apps as "not really games" there is still a lot to be learned from them about what the audience of Facebook wants from their interaction in the Facebook Instant Games space:

1. Quick effortless interaction
2. Personalised shares that the user feels they can be represented by
3. Easy access and visibility of the games to players to remind them they even exist

The environment of each social app and social media at large is perpetually changing, and the truth is we don't know exactly what shape it will all take in the next five or ten years. I suspect that there will always be an appetite for different kinds of entertainment on the different platforms, and trends and games will come and go. Whether games scholars would classify these as "games" or "playful experiences" matters less, and what matters is that we learn little by little from each of them and use that knowledge to build ever-improving social experiences, as we will elaborate in later chapters.

The death of Facebook social games as they used to be gave birth to an opportunity for different kinds of social experiences to be created, and many studios are still figuring it out. I believe that now that the internet has entered a more mature phase and Moore's law is slowing. We will see less shifting in the tech itself and as a result game makers will push the limits of interaction design when the waters of ever-evolving tech calm down a little.

Notes

1. Peter Suciu, "Gen Z Not 'Friending' On Facebook – How Will The Social Network Respond?" *Forbes*, 6 September 2022, https://www.forbes.com/sites/petersuciu/2022/09/06/gen-z-not-friending-on-facebookhow-will-the-social-network-respond/.
2. Statista. "UK Facebook users by age group 2023." Statista, 22 May 2023, https://www.statista.com/statistics/1030055/facebook-users-united-kingdom/. Accessed 11 November 2023.
3. Statista. "U.S. Facebook user activities 2020." Statista, 28 April 2022, https://www.statista.com/statistics/275788/share-of-facebook-user-activities/. Accessed 11 November 2023.
4. Jason Rubin, "Changes to the Instant Games Platform", *Facebook*, 2020, https://www.facebook.com/fbgaminghome/blog/changes-to-the-instant-games-platform.

Part 3

---

*Social game design for a
modern audience*

chapter 6

Experimenting with social mechanics

Early social games on Facebook managed to use social features to gain traction and longevity, but the way we use the internet to communicate has changed a lot since then. The popularity of smartphones and the ubiquity of the internet changed how frequent and immediate our experience with social media was. Because of these changes, applying the same social features in the same way early social games did will not lead to the same results in today's ecosystem. The only way to go about it is to test these social mechanics and in the process build an understanding of the audience and how they like to use the platform they are on. Social game mechanics are difficult to get right because they ask the player to involve their social network in order to achieve something in the game. So naturally, players will be engaging in these mechanics only as far as the social contract permits them.

The process of testing many of these mechanics was long and laborious. For some of the features, we discovered it was the platform that determined whether or not they worked, while for others it was all about the audience and how they use social media presently as opposed to back then. But in order to understand what worked and what didn't, it's worth having a very clear understanding of the structure of the different kinds of social mechanics and what kind of purpose they fulfil. In the rest of this chapter I will break down the different kinds of social mechanics and endeavour to explain how the use of them changed through time and from one generation of players to the next.

Social mechanics: What are they and how to use them

To start, it is best to define what I understand "social mechanics" to be because in my opinion the term is a lot more broad than the kind of mechanics used in social games or mobile games and extends to other multiplayer games as well. I would therefore define it as "a game mechanic that has the player socially engage with others, where the ultimate goal can be either social connection or mechanical gain as a result of complex social interaction". This implies two main things. Firstly, it establishes that

DOI: 10.1201/9781003314325-9

for a mechanic to be social either the ultimate goal must be to socially connect or that the social interaction must be complex. Secondly, it includes
social interaction both with other players and with people outside the
game, which is important to encompass features that extend beyond the
boundaries of the game.

Social connection takes multiple forms, all of them derived from the
way that humans create bonds with each other and what they do to establish and maintain those bonds. As a result, the social mechanic can then
be categorised by what social goal they ultimately aim to fulfil:

- **Sense of presence**: Players get to feel like they are in the same space
  at the same time connecting socially with people. This most commonly takes the form of synchronous features, seeing avatars in the
  same virtual space, being able to interact with other people's avatars
  or even seeing a friend's Facebook profile picture on a saga map.
- **Relationship exploration**: Players get to learn more about themselves, other people and their relationships. These can take the
  form of asymmetric gameplay mechanics, but more literally about
  mechanics that aim to see how and if another person responds such
  as asking for help or sending a "do you know me" question.
- **Proof of relationship**: Players get one way or another to prove their
  relationship with another person. This can range from mechanics
  such as gifting or sending help, but it also includes things like relationship statuses.
- **Show of status**: Players get to showcase their skills or what they
  have to others. This most commonly takes the form of leaderboard
  shares or other types of proof of performance, but it can also take
  the form of sharing player creations and showcasing their creativity.

On the other hand, players can also interact with a social feature for
mechanical gain in which case the mechanics being considered social are
defined by the core of the interaction being of social nature even if the goal
is mechanical. This includes mechanics like trading or competing with
other players for a reward.

As you can probably tell, a lot of modern games employ at least one
of these mechanics. The reality is that the line between what is called
a "social game" and what is just considered a "multiplayer" game has
become very blurry. In the beginning, the limitations of the platforms
gave birth to a quite different style of game most of the time predominantly revolving around async multiplayer, as we previously discussed,
but that is no longer the case. Not only is this new generation of social
games capable of so much more in the ways of multiplayer (covering a
spectrum of sync and async features) but with apps expanding to be more
multipurpose it's hard to clearly categorise what is a social game based

solely on its presence on a social platform. This is why I felt the need to make a definition for a social mechanic that is more inclusive and relies on the actual social interaction rather than its association with social media or the kind of social mechanics one would have seen in an old Facebook game.

Multiplayer

Multiplayer comes in two very distinct forms: synchronous (sync) and asynchronous (async). These two types of multiplayer are not new or unique to video games. A football game, for example, could be technically seen as synchronous multiplayer, since the game needs all the players to be in the same place at the same time in order to take place. Asynchronous, on the other hand, does not have to be played at the same time. Although a bit of an antiquated example we can think of any type of "play-by-mail" game. Before the internet, people used to play a lot of turn-based games by mail, things like war games or even long-distance chess.

While certain games might have a harder or easier time being played in either a sync or an async format based on the core mechanic, they are not in opposition with each other but rather just different ways of establishing and sustaining that social connection. For example, a predominantly synchronous multiplayer game might include asynchronous features in order to offer different levels of interaction to the players, something that can be done between the sessions when not everyone is available to play. Similarly, a predominantly async game might add a synchronous feature to show when others are online and what they are doing in order to amplify that feeling of presence. There is no real reason to limit ourselves to one aspect of multiplayer, instead we can tailor the kind of multiplayer interaction we have in the game to the goals and desires of the audience.

Both of these types of multiplayer come with advantages and disadvantages as you might expect. Synchronous multiplayer is high intensity and high commitment for the player. It requires scheduling, coordination and communication, and it implies a certain degree of performance on behalf of those involved because everyone is present and watching. In return for this intensity, this type of multiplayer has a very high presence, meaning that those involved really feel like they are hanging out with their friends socially and making memories together. On the other hand, asynchronous is lower intensity and lower commitment, making it perfect for those who want to play a game more casually or do not have time and energy to engage with a game in this more intense way. In return, however, the feeling of presence is much reduced because there is just not the same feeling of virtually inhabiting the same place at the same time.

Early social games preferred asynchronous features over synchronous partially due to some technical limitations but predominantly because their audience did not have as much appetite for intense interaction. Casual Facebook game players preferred to log in for a certain amount of time at specific times a day to play their game without having to coordinate with others when to do so. This mirrors the use pattern of Facebook and unsurprisingly this is what we found across the different platforms I have had the chance to work on during my career in social games.

On Facebook Messenger, the audience was not very interested in sync multiplayer. The experiments we have done with different types of synchronous mechanics at varying levels of intensity showed that people were just not interested in it. They used Facebook Messenger as a replacement for SMS and they did not expect or want to spend long amounts of time in the app to try or coordinate with other people to play a game at the same time. Instead they preferred games that could be picked up and put down immediately at any time, much like responding to a message someone sent. The structure of Facebook Instant Games on Messenger games resembled the way people were already using the platform. This is why async multiplayer features thrived on the platform, the idea being that anyone can drop in at any time, leave something for their friend and exit was perfect for them. This resulted in a lot of back-and-forth notification play inside a conversation keeping the other players apprised of what was happening and creating something similar to a gameplay thread inside the conversation window.

Games in Snapchat on the other hand behaved quite differently. Not entirely dissimilar to Facebook Messenger users, Snapchatters did not spend a long amount of time in the app in one go, opening and closing it frequently. However, the behaviour of the users around app notifications was very different and changed drastically in the kind of game that would be played on the platform. At the time we were developing for Snapchat, the app was already notifying its users when a friend started typing in a chat. This meant that the feeling of Snapchat was more synchronous overall even if the moments of synchronicity were brief. This meant that players were open to playing at the same time and dropping in to join a friend for a quick match because they were used to being notified of their friend's activity and joining them briefly before continuing with their day. Asynchronous features were not the main attraction for these games, instead they served as supporting features for the sync multiplayer, and there were two main reasons for it. Firstly and most importantly was the ephemerality of the platform. Messages are not meant to last in a conversation on Snapchat, this is why a game thread like the one we spoke about in the case of Facebook Messenger would not be suitable. Secondly, async by itself was a little bit too low frequency for Snapchat users. A turn-based game played over a long period of time was not what they were looking for, favouring instead short bursts of fun gameplay that they could start and finish quickly.

The platform Discord is even more different still. Players are used to coming together to the platform to hang out in a voice channel and either watch someone play or do some other activity together. This means that time spent inside the game is longer and that they favour activities that are synchronous for the sense of presence that it gives the group since the work of coming together is something they are already used to doing on the platform. Asynchronous features are something we are still exploring on this platform at the time of writing this book, but although I can totally see them being easier to engage with in a way that they could not be on Snapchat due to its ephemerality, Discord so far remains a predominantly synchronous multiplayer platform.

Be it sync or async, multiplayer still relies on other people responding in a timely manner. Synchronous response happens before the joint play session. This means that a "timely answer" in this case means the window in which the initiating player is available to play. Asynchronous is a little more forgiving in this sense. The initiating player can start a joint session and the "timely answer" in this case is represented by the interest of the other player in playing the game in their own time. Sometimes a response from a friend might reignite interest in the game even if the response comes a while after the initial invitation to play.

The difficulties posed by this need for a timely answer is a very important and tricky problem to solve, and depending on the ultimate goal of the game there are different ways to approach this problem. One method would be to deprioritise multiplayer in favour of single player and make playing with others an additive feature in order to hook the initiating player and give them something to engage with while they are waiting for their friend. This means that they will only access the multiplayer feature when they can get other people to join them. This is not a bad idea, but in this case the core of the game is no longer social multiplayer but a single-player game with added multiplayer components. Another way to deal with this same issue is to make the game always multiplayer but offer a multitude of other ways to play it, be it against bots or against strangers. This method keeps the core of the game focused on the multiplayer, but it has its drawbacks. Bots are oftentimes not a good substitute for a real player because while mechanically suitable there is no human connection. But just the same, always playing against other people and especially people we do not know can be very high intensity for someone who wants to play casually. The last option is to make a game that accommodates any number of players and keep it fluid. This is a bit of a hybrid between the other two methods, meaning the initiating player can still play by themselves, but the moment the other person responds they can flawlessly transition to playing in multiplayer. This method is ideal for keeping the core of the game flexible and keeping the attention on the multiplayer aspects of the game, but by nature of its flexibility it has added logistical challenges that the other methods do not have to deal with. The difficulties vary from issues of fairness when we are talking about player versus player (PvP), to issues of balancing when it comes to making a game that is suitably difficult for one person but scaled to allow multiple players to the actual technical difficulty of having a game that allows a player to just spawn in the same place at the same time potentially without a very rigid matchmaking structure.

The answer to how one game deals with its multiplayer and the rigidity or not of the structure remains up to the game. What we have found time and time again is that multiplayer for these different social and messenger platforms has to be as frictionless as possible because these people are there to socialise first and play second. This means that players want to join their friends right away, they do not want to wait to have fun and be involved with what is happening. Waiting in a lobby in this case is out of the question. Similarly, being able to make one move in a turn base, send a request and then wait for a friend to respond is not enough to entertain. There has to be more to the game that keeps the player engaged even when their friends cannot respond to their request.

We also found that across platforms there is no real substitute for playing with other humans. We found that while bots are useful to fill in the gaps when needed, players can see through them immediately and they cannot be used as any kind of longer-term solution. Players learn the patterns of the AI and they tend to get bored of playing against them, especially if playing with or against bots is not a deliberate option the player makes but rather something that happens when there are no real players to play with. Matching with strangers was in fact a lot more popular than we expected on these platforms given the idea that these environments are spaces for people to communicate with others they already knew. Not only did these people prefer engaging with other humans that they did not know, but they also often wanted to connect with those other players outside the game when the game went well. There is an interesting conversation to be had when we are talking about games on social platforms and "strangers", oftentimes regarding issues of safeguarding and privacy. Different platforms have different rules regarding the player befriending someone they don't know outside the game, but that does not dissuade people.

In the end we found it was important to allow for flexibility and make it so that the player is the one who feels in charge of their experience, especially when it comes to playing with others. And however challenging that flexibility was to maintain, it did ultimately create an environment that suited whatever the user had going on in their own social life, which was ultimately the most important for us.

Social metagame and larger groups

While different kinds of multiplayer concern themselves with the core loop of the game and the way that players interact with each other to complete it, the social metagame is the layer on top of the game that encourages the players to collaborate on longer-term goals. Most of the time the social metagame takes the form of asynchronous features, which gives players the flexibility necessary to cooperate without having to be engaged in synchronous play.

The social metagame uses group-based mechanics that can serve many purposes:

- Giving players a sense of community and communal achievement, for example, joining a guild/faction or engaging in a community-wide event
- Offering players an opportunity to challenge other players and prove themselves, for example, engaging with leagues and leaderboards
- Encouraging players to build or create with others, such as creating an in-game trading market or having community-wide goals

Most of these mechanics are widely used in all kinds of games from your usual well-featured mobile game to the more hardcore PC and console multiplayer that most commonly run in LiveOps. All of these games employ group mechanics to enrich the game experience and to keep the community engaged until the next update comes along.

A social meta can be incredibly powerful when done right. but it's important to know that in order for the player to care and engage with this type of mechanics they have to already be quite involved with the game. Throughout the lifetime of playing a game, the player's social interests are likely to expand or change. At first the player is too concerned with their own performance; they need to understand how to play a game before they can engage with others in any social mechanical way. This is true even in the case where players start playing as part of a pair or a group, because while technically part of a social situation the individual will not be able to fully engage with others until they understand the core of the game. For some games, this first step is easy due to the familiarity or the simplicity of the main mechanic. The players must first establish a virtual identity (as we spoke of previously) and understand themselves in the context of the game. Once the player has established enough control and feels confident in their skills of playing, they can then engage with the next level of the social meta.

The next level of the social meta is embracing the position of the player within a group in a mechanical context. This takes the form of intragroup strategy; it involves reading and understanding other people's play habits and abilities. In this case, strategy can take many forms, from finding out how best to support your team in a MOBA (multiplayer online battle arena) to finding out what gets the most laughs in a game like Gartic Phone. This stage is not about the complexity of the game as much as it is about the complexity of our social positioning inside the game and forming that virtual social identity we spoke of. Most commonly at this stage players will engage with the people they already know and feel comfortable with. At this point the player is still mostly concerned with their own performance, but their play is being framed in the context of a group. Only if and when the player is comfortable with their place in this group are they finally ready to engage with the community at large, sometimes on their own, other times as a representation of the group they have previously established.

The final tier and the top of the social meta is interaction with the community. This happens when the player is so confident in their ability with the game both in a personal context and in a social context that they are happy to engage with others outside of their immediate circle. This can be a daunting experience and some players may never reach a level in which this kind of interaction is comfortable to them even if there are plenty of mechanical benefits encouraging them.

The significance of each of the three tiers is not always equal in every game, but the order in which they are present is always the same and I would posit that not skipping the different levels of social interaction makes for a more successful transition for the player from a beginner, concerned with their own performance, to long-term power player involved socially in the wider game community (Figure 6.1).

It is also worth noting that it is not guaranteed that players will move from one layer of social interaction to the other on their own. Some might be naturally more inclined to do so and progress quickly, others might take a very long time before they reach the final milestone. Some might consider the interaction with the community too much involvement for issues of perceived skill, have concerns about privacy or even lack of desire to interact with others that are not their immediate group. This is why understanding how much interaction with the community the audience is ready to have is fundamental. Offering them something that is highly connected might be theoretically the "best way" to get social interaction with the community, but if the majority of the people are not happy to engage with the game the point of it becomes moot.

When done correctly in a way that players will want to engage with, community mechanics can expand the social play experience tremendously by facilitating players to get involved in something bigger than their immediate group.

Guild or faction competitions and leaderboards elevate the concept of best performance to something more akin to a football league; the player is a puzzle piece to the success of the team. And much like in football the players need to individually perform at their best to ensure success, but they also need to cooperate and put the needs of the group before their own. This also goes back to what we discussed in the first chapter: large group mechanics rely on the social obligation to make them work. This is precisely why players should engage with it at their own pace.

Player is concerned with their place in the community

How do my group and I contribute to the community?

Player is concerned with their performance within the group

How do I cooperate with others?

Player is concerned with their own performance

How do I play this game?

Figure 6.1 The pyramid of player social interest

Although community mechanics are fascinating and they have been proven to work in multiple circumstances, there are also significant challenges to building such systems. First, the player has to see some value in engaging in group mechanics beyond just the regular in-game rewards. This is because it requires more social and emotional energy to operate as part of a large group. They need to understand the social implications of joining a guild/faction, and they need to adjust their strategy to accommodate the goal of the group while simultaneously leaving themselves open up for scrutiny and rejection should they not perform at the level the group expects them to. This kind of dynamic is what makes larger groups so interesting, but it also makes them intimidating, especially for those who are only engaged in a game on a casual level.

An interesting case study for this is *Pokémon GO*, which launched with a three-faction competition, from the get-go asking people to join the game as part of a faction. What this ultimately led to was players wanting to be part of the dominant faction, defending their choices and contributing through gameplay to this worldwide competition. People would engage in discourse on social media about the subject and try to convince their friends to join their faction. How did this work in the case of *Pokémon GO* if the players did not have the chance to rise through the different levels of interactions we previously spoke about? The answer is more complex, but it ultimately boils down to two things: intuitive mechanics and devotion to the IP. Most players had a previous emotional attachment to the fantasy the game was selling; this paired with the intuitive gameplay allowed the players to engage with the community a lot easier. However, for a game that does not benefit from the fame and fandom of a large IP, it is best to allow people to accommodate the social idea of playing in a small group first, to get them involved with the idea of playing with people before even showing them the option to be part of something bigger.

Community mechanics can take many forms and they are preferred by different kinds of players with different levels of involvement with the game.

- **Leaderboards and high-score tables**: Players don't have to do anything to be part of a community-wide competition; they are in it by default. They may or may not care about it when they first join the game, but the option is there if/when they decide to. This is the most frictionless way to do this, but it is also rather impersonal as far as community interaction goes.
- **Guilds and factions**: Players may choose to join a guild and their experience as part of the group is entirely additive to the player's experience of playing the game alone or with friends. Guilds are there to be a net positive experience for the player, meaning that they get rewarded for the achievements of the group and do not get "punished" for any failings of said group. Guilds can be involved in community-wide competitions with each other or just have collective goals and rewards.
- **Ranked matches and tournaments**: Players engage in high-tension PvP as an individual or a team in a way that classifies them for a community competition that is opt-in by way of playing a specific type of PvP.
- **Community seasonal goals**: Players can engage in community-wide seasonal events in order to unlock limited-time content, where the determining factor of the unlock is the progress of the group and not that of the individual.

Community features benefit from longer-term social goals, on the scale of weeks, months or seasons. This is why all of these features are asynchronous even if to engage with them one must first play the game synchronously with other people (like in the case of ranked matches). This is because the larger the group of players we aim to mobilise, the more difficult it is to do so in a short period of time.

Something we have noticed when testing different community features was that people playing together in small groups tend to think of themselves as a unit when playing against others. They enjoyed engaging in competition inside the group at times, but when it came to them being part of a larger community, the individual identified with their smaller group and would engage with others as such. This speaks to that group identity who is the individual inside a group and how they see themselves as being part of said group.

Another fascinating facet of community mechanics is the amount of developer-imposed regulation regarding the running of the group. While self-regulating communities require less work on behalf of the developer, it's easy to see why a free-for-all is not actually a good idea. Players should have enough freedom in managing and engaging with their group so they feel like they can create an organic connection, but it's also a developer's responsibility to manage and control group dynamics to ensure one player's enjoyment of the game isn't ruining the experience for everyone else.

When creating a game where player-to-player interaction is desirable, at different levels the amount of control we have over the way the community interacts can make or break the overall atmosphere. This brings practical issues of privacy into question such as what kind of information can I see about others and what information they can see about me, but it's also a question of ethics such as how do we manage a community without forcing people into relationship boxes that we create. In Chapter 9 I will go more in depth into the role game creators play in people's relationships when making a game intended for social interaction and how to navigate that space with ethics in mind.

Sharing

The mechanic of sharing game snippets to the internet has been around long before social media with people posting their game experiences in forums online, but in more recent times a lot of games have seen the value in making the sharing of game content easier. The idea of a way to easily share game content outside the game originated with the early Facebook games and soon after a lot of mobile games adopted the mechanic. Nowadays even console and PC games have embraced the idea that sharing is desirable and gaming systems go as far as to have a button on the controller for easy recording and sharing of content. Content shares help with a sense of community by allowing players to easily communicate with others about the game outside of it and encourage the virality of the game by increasing its visibility.

Sharing is part of being human; it revolves around our need to have common experiences with those we love in order to create empathy with one another. Sharing video game content is driven by the same desire to share any personal information or achievement. It's a reflection of who the person is and what they are interested in, and it's being put out in a desire to get people to interact and associate with the sharer. Paradoxically, people share content not only to engage with others and find kinship, but also to show their unique personalities and achievements. It's as much about being a member of the group as it is about being a unique individual.

In the specific context of a social mechanic in a video game, sharing is a way to distribute game content outside of the game itself, not just on social media, although most commonly those are the platforms easiest to link to. Furthermore, a sharing feature aims to give the player easy access to capture an aspect of the game and post the resulting content to an external source without fully stopping the game experience.

The content being posted can take many forms and will always end up being heavily influenced by the platform it is being shared to. This is because, by definition, this kind of feature is there to translate something the game can output into something the other platform (social media) can host. More often than not it's the destination platform that decides the format of a share, and they do so in accordance with what their audience is already used to consuming on said platform.

Shares can be categorised in a few different ways, one way is to look at them based on their purpose at their destination (i.e. what is the share trying to instil in the people who are the receiving end of the share). The other way to look at this is through the lens of the person choosing to do the share in the first place and their motivation (i.e. what is the motivation the sender has to take this action).

When it comes to categorising shares based on their purpose at the destination, I would say there are two main types:

- **Virality-focused/ad-like shares**: These shares are usually destined for a large audience, so the content is less specific. The point of the share is to intrigue and to make those who have not seen or played the game before to consider giving it a go. To achieve this, viral shares need to connect to social platform features that allow exposure to multiple people in one go (e.g. a person's Facebook wall) or a feature that makes sharing to multiple individuals at the same time easy (e.g. sharing to multiple people the same content in separate chats). Virality shares are similar to ads in format, but they can be a lot more targeted since they are coming from a friend. We can present a share as an invite to help or a challenge sent by the player to their friends (e.g. "X needs another farm in their village", "X ran 245 metres, can you do better?"). It's important to remember that the person sharing needs to be in agreement with the content of the share; this is both for ethical and efficiency reasons. Users are more savvy than ever; they understand that sharing is essentially a form of endorsement for the game, therefore, trying to "trick" them will not work and it will also make the player not trust the game in the future. Later I will go over the user's motivations to share as well.

- **Reengagement focused/notification-like shares**: These shares are highly specific, often aimed at a single person or members of the same group. Traditionally, these kinds of shares are connected to private means of conversation between users (i.e. private messages between people). This type of share also assumes that the sender and the receiver have already established an in-game relationship, so the share's goal is less to intrigue and more to inform and remind. These shares can be highly personalised and they can also be more frequent without causing fatigue to the receiver. To make sure these shares are received well they still need to be able to catch the eye of the receiver, but the content should be less general and more informative (e.g. "HELP! X needs 200 stones to finish the village well").

Another way to look at shares is by what drives the sender to share in the first place. While the receiver's categorisations tell us more about how shares should be presented at their destinations, this tells us more about how they should be presented and incentivised inside the game. Understanding the player's motivations for sharing helps us not only optimise how frequently the users do it, but it also helps us establish a relationship with the player. This is because we want the player to not only understand exactly what the share will do and look like once out in the wild, but we actually want them to desire sharing and not see the feature as a cheap form of advertisement. Content that is willingly shared by a player to their social network has higher chances of engaging recipients, especially those in close circles with the sender because they feel more like a personal note and less like a generic ad. This is how shares are divided based on the sender's motivation:

- **Incentivised shares**: This type of share is the most common and unfortunately it's also the least interesting to the player. The idea behind them is very simple: we treat the whole experience as a transaction between the player and the game. This type of share relies on the player being involved enough with the game that they consider in-game rewards a fair exchange for an endorsement. However, because of the nature of incentivised shares, they are harder to personalise and therefore less likely to elicit a response from recipients. The best way to use this kind of share is to add incentives on top of another type of share to make it even more attractive to the user.
- **Vanity shares**: This type of share is often used in games that have a strong competitive component, but they are not limited to competitive games. The intention is to allow the player to showcase their

achievements. Depending on the player and the game this means different things. Some players enjoy showcasing how good they are at the game; this means sharing high scores, leaderboard positions or other performance metrics. For the more creative players, vanity sharing is all about self-expression; they want to share what they built or accumulated and pride themselves in the way their influence on the game has created a unique thing. Discovery-oriented players pride themselves on finding new and rare things; they want to talk about the obscure elements of the game that they discovered and others might not know about. Social players take pride in relating their actions to other people they know; they are most likely to share moments where they had an interaction with someone else (e.g. "overtaking a friend on the leaderboard", "completing a task a friend needed help with"). The trick with vanity shares is to make them available to the player whenever there is an opportunity but not force them to share. This way each player can make their own decisions about what they would like to put out and the share will be more authentic.

- **Social connection shares**: This type of share is motivated solely because of the social value they bring the player. In this case, the person doing the sharing is looking for kinship and interaction with others as a primary reward. This may mean they are trying to share something relatable or funny or will bring them sympathy from others.
- **Gameplay-facilitating shares**: This type of share is by far the most practical because they are there to enhance gameplay and offer the player an accessible tool to bring their friends in to help or to challenge. Unlike the incentivise share that offers the player sharing a reward that can help them mechanically, a gameplay-facilitating share is more complex; it's more or less a call to join multiplayer that is specifically focusing on a task at hand (e.g. X wants to challenge you to 1v1 [one versus one] match).
- **Updates and automatic notifications**: This type of share is akin to periodically posted status updates, aimed to inform others of the player's activity in the game. Because these shares are automatic, instead of having to convince the player to take action, the game must convince the player not to take action against it and turn the notifications off. A lot of the older style of async multiplayer functioned primarily through the method of back-and-forth automatic notifications about the other player. However, in more recent times this kind of share is seen as spammy and is now often limited by rules against posting anything on behalf of the player, and they have slowly become obsolete because of said regulations.

The appeal and format of shares changed throughout the existence of the "share" as a social mechanic. While some of it is due to new rules and regulations imposed on social platforms, some of them come from the audience's preference and appetite for different kinds of self-expression as well as their desire to cultivate a virtual social image. In the following chapters I will discuss in more detail how the current market engages with social mechanics, what has changed and why.

Discovering the social mechanics for the next generation

In the journey of finding solid design pillars and a formula for what we call hyper-social games (the newer generation of social games), there has been a lot of experimentation that yielded quite frequently unexpected results. This is because the audience we were looking at serving is savvy with technology, the internet was more mature than when our social game predecessors were making waves and the sociocultural climate changed rapidly in the time after the social media boom of the early to mid-2010s. Back in 2008 when Facebook started to become popular, the whole concept of a smartphone was very much a novelty, so people didn't have access to the internet and their feeds everywhere they went. The targeted ads scene was also very different; the internet was still young and while there were concerns about privacy in the minds of those who knew how these systems were working, that concern was far from the minds of the average user of these social networks. People treated Facebook as a novelty to be experimented with and an easy way to broadcast anything and everything. People did not expect the longevity of these posts and many did not consider the long-term repercussions to their long-term image. It felt like in a few years the internet went from being a place of anonymous personas and pseudonyms to a place where people displayed their full real name and shared their every move. The transparency of it and the lack of rules were partly what created the environment in which social games of a specific format could thrive.

This environment, however, changed rapidly and by the late 2010s we were looking at a completely different scene. Users, especially Gen Z, understand very clearly what it means to create and keep an online persona, to the degree that they curate different online identities on these platforms to appeal to different groups of people. They are also increasingly more concerned about privacy and data gathering and the laws protecting personal data have become a lot more precise. While it sounds like this would hinder social games, it is not at all like that; these savvy users are incredibly open to using social networks, but they just want to do it on their own terms. I believe this to be a very healthy way of approaching social gaming and social media in general, and this shift was inevitable and necessary as the internet matured.

New social media shifted in their purpose to match this new way of thinking about the internet:

- They focus on fewer connections but closer ones with real friends rather than broadcasting to many people ("real friends" here refers to the strength of their bond rather than to "real life" friendships).
- They are less focused on likes and more focused on more expressive interaction: reactions, comments, responses.
- They focus on bite-size content, and even though there is a lot to consume it's deliberately short-form.

In the next chapter I will be covering in more detail the things that work well for hyper-social games. But before we move on to that I wanted to highlight some of the things that we experimented with that didn't end up working:

- Traditional multiplayer lobby structures are too slow for them. This audience is used to things being instantaneous; they like to connect with each other immediately. Waiting for rigid match structures and cumbersome lobbies does not suit the way that they like to interact with their friends.
- Async is not enough. Players want to feel like their friends are present in the game at the same time, even if the game is turn-based, they prefer games that have synchronous features if multiple players happen to be online at the same time.
- Too much coordination can be detrimental. For making this kind of game it is worth mentioning that players are there to socialise first and play second. This means that while there has to be a degree of coordination between players, there also has to be a degree of lightness to these games so players have the mental space to socially engage with those they are playing with.
- Spamming the player does not bring them back, instead they are more likely to block notifications. This is a very tight line to walk, but it is very important. The online world of today is so incredibly noisy that people will silence notifications that are not useful to them because they drown out the things they actually care about.

How best to learn from players: Interview with Jen Bolton

Jen Bolton and I have been working really closely to make sure that we approach the process of designing for the audience with compassion. Aside from the obvious numbers game we all play, there is a more human quality to learning from players that I believe we all need to know about. Working with Jen really helped me understand the best methods of learning from players, and we worked as a team to put that learning to good use. While I have covered some of the things I have learned from her throughout this book and especially in this chapter, I thought it was best to hear her perspective as well on these topics. In this interview we discuss more about the role of a user researcher and what that work entails, and we also speak about the differences between generations and where we think the internet is heading.

Jen Bolton: So I'm Jen. I am the VP of Player Insights at Mojiworks, which is pretty much my dream job. It's my first job that is all about user research, although I've done research here and there throughout my career. In this role, I'm a player liaison, so I'm the voice of the game and the company to our players. I'm also a player advocate, so I help the development team to understand the experiences of players, their preferences and what they're looking for in games. We're always looking to find out more about the audience in our team. And so you know that I have a pivotal role in finding out what motivates players socially.

I'm also a community manager, probably a little more than that now. I started doing this sort of thing when I first found the internet in the mid-'90s, before you could see images on web pages. I was in chat rooms a lot and I met a lot of people online who are still in my life now and one of them is my husband. So the internet has always been about people for me. So I think it was kind of a natural progression for me to end up working in this field.

After initially working in a bunch of office management roles, I worked for Virgin Clothing company. And that's when my break was, when blogging started to become a thing. I created an online portal, the first portal for blogging in the UK and it was called GBlogs. And I met a lot of people online then, who are still my friends and who are spread out around the world.

Later I joined Stor Entertainment, a startup that made online and community software and offered services for entertainment companies, including Warner Brothers and Channel 4. There I managed online forums and celebrity live chats for Channel 4. We did a lot of fun community stuff back when not a lot of people were doing it. Channel 4 was really innovative in that way. But then the dotcom bubble burst and unfortunately, we all went our separate ways. I decided to have a baby, so I took a little bit of time off and kind of went into the charity sector for a bit.

And then when my daughter was about three, one of my friends from the UK blogging community said, "I got a job and I think you'd be perfect for it. Are you looking to go back to work?" This was a job heading the online community department for NCSoft in Brighton. We were looking after all of NCSoft's games released in Europe (*City of Heroes*, *Guild Wars* and a few others). I was very daunted by this. I never worked in games before, but I absolutely loved games my whole life. This was a convergence of a bunch of things at a very scary time because I was a new parent. But needless to say, I went for that job, and I went from being a full-time mom to representing millions and millions of players across Europe.

My role at NCSoft was very much managerial; I had 11 direct reports. We were one of the first games companies that I know of to be on Facebook. We also did interesting things on Twitter. My job was to champion and empower our community managers and I really enjoyed those few years and those people. Most of the people I managed have gone on to have really incredible careers as games developers, marketers and online community specialists.

How it started out on Facebook was more about broadcasting to a larger and larger audience compared to the more niche forums I worked on, but now it has come full circle with apps like Snapchat, TikTok and Discord kind of making things a bit more small groupie again. So seeing the progression of it and being able to work through all of the incarnations of that has been really fascinating.

Ioana-Iulia Cazacu: You were talking about how this is actually your first proper job in research, but I know that you have studied psychology as well. I was wondering if that was something you always wanted to do or something that you discovered through doing community management.

Jen Bolton: Behavioural psychology has always fascinated me. I don't know why I didn't start out doing a degree in psychology way back when, but I went for English instead. It took me 26 years to finish my undergrad degree. I hopped around a lot, but social science with a psychology degree had all the elements that I was really interested in. At the time when I started at NCSoft I decided that there is an awful lot going on here and that I want to understand it all and go about it in a more methodical way. So I wanted a solid grounding in psychological principles and that degree helped me an awful lot.

For my final project I ran interviews with people in the games industry to uncover their ideas about gender and in how that kind of surfaces in the way people talk about games and gamers. I got very in depth about the actual words and speech patterns, which I loved analysing. Something illuminating coming out of it was that it's not only what people will say and how they say it, but also the gaps in between and what they're not saying. When you record someone for an interview you're looking for those things in a transcript, and it feels like you're uncovering secrets. It's like easter eggs in people's communication. Checking that back with the interviewees afterwards and showing them these things was fascinating and they were surprised by some of the stuff they "said" and had genuine aha moments.

Using these principles to be able to tell stories about player experiences, I'm having so much fun doing it and I think it's really valuable for the teams I work with, and I think as time goes by more things are coming together.

Ioana-Iulia Cazacu: You mentioned that you were a fan of games growing up and that they played an important role throughout your entire life. So when the opportunity came along, you were really excited about working in the gaming sector. Can you tell us more about your own history of playing games with other people?

Jen Bolton: I first started being interested in games as a little kid in the '70s. We had handheld games; we didn't yet have Atari. One of my earliest memories is of fighting with my brother over the handheld Tron, which only one of us could play at a time. But we both sit there together and watch each other play. So it was kind of social even though, you know, we weren't playing multiplayer.

I didn't really start playing games with friends until the Atari 2600 came out. In the beginning I was very much a solo gamer playing the Infocom text adventures by myself at the time you couldn't really play multiplayer games.

When I was about ten, I remember the Pizza Hut near my neighbourhood in New York having a tabletop *Space Invaders* game where you could sit at it and play. My family would go there every so often. That felt like, "Wow, it's like we're playing a board game, except it's a video game". But until like the 2600 and console games, the socialness of games was real life.

My first experience of a massively multiplayer online game was *World of Warcraft*. I played multiplayer games online. That was the first time I met people online that I didn't already know in real life through a game. That was very cool and some of them I'm still in touch with. So I guess I kind of did it all.

Ioana-Iulia Cazacu: Every time I ask the interviewee this question we always circle back to the same discussion about games being a social event even when they cannot be physically played in a multiplayer way.

Jen Bolton: It's really about sharing something you love with people, right? And this is what the internet facilitated in the end, is one of the reasons I do what I do.

Ioana-Iulia Cazacu: Going on from that I would like it if we could go a little bit back and talk about communities given your experience. You touched upon earlier about the way people like to communicate online (going from at some point in the past in large groups may be more performative, and more recently noticing the preference for smaller communities and groups). I was wondering if you could tell us more about how people's attitudes towards online communities have changed over time.

Jen Bolton: Oh wow, that's a fun question. I think some of it is kind of generational. I was online before AOL slightly, which was the first thing in the US that brought people in an instant messenger. ICQ was another one and other early programs, some more user-friendly alternatives for people to chat online and all of it was based around smaller groups or pairs. I think that was most people's first experience of this kind at that particular time. Most of them were coming online and finding the novelty of being able to communicate with the same people you would every day but in this new way.

Then social networks started to emerge. The first one I actually remember was classmates.com. That was a US-based site to help you find your old high school friends. It was terrible to use. But everybody was on there because we were all really interested in knowing what the people that we knew from school were doing. It was mostly driven by curiosity. They also pitched themselves as the place to organise your high school reunion. Then LiveJournal happened and Myspace. These platforms had terrible interfaces but people still found their way to them usually through their university accounts, like I did. People started to build their own spaces online much easier.

The reason it all worked so well is it solved that frustration for people by just having everything in one place. Also getting over the difficulty of making our own website even though platforms like GeoCities and Yahoo really tried to make that happen. But for those the learning curve was just too steep for most people. So it made sense that something like Myspace would get a lot of traction fast and it did. We saw this in the blogging community as well. I coded my own blog online in HTML and CSS, but then Blogger.com came along and a couple of other alternatives to it. People started using those platforms moving away from their own thing, also because of convenience.

I think with both of these, the social networks and the blogs, people liked the novelty of having an audience. When Facebook emerged as a contender the world got interested in it because it was better put together than Myspace. It was less US-centric and it was friendlier to use. When I was working with NCSoft, Facebook grew really fast, and people started realising that they had an audience beyond the people that they already knew, and suddenly everyone could have wider influence. You could meet more people like yourself and put more of yourself out there. Nobody was thinking about privacy concerns. In the background, all of the data gathering was happening that very few people were actually aware of.

The shift back to smaller groups, close-friend-oriented platforms and privacy was fuelled by the issue around data gathering. From the early days of Facebook people started to feel uncomfortable with everyone knowing everything about them. And the laws changed to try to prevent abuse of people's personal information. Younger people who have always been online will never know what life on the internet was before.

Their struggles however have been really different and I watch my own child go through this. I haven't exactly navigated it with her, but she had parents that both existed and worked online for decades and who understand this stuff pretty thoroughly. So I think she's probably a bit atypical of people her age; she never put herself that much online. She was quite protective of her image and so was I from the time when she was born. I didn't even use her name online. I didn't ever want to manage that for her. I knew she would inevitably have a digital identity and I wanted that to be owned by her. So I was custodian of it for the first 12 years of her life, then I explained to her how the internet is the best and worst of humanity. This is why she was very cautious about it and I think she'll be glad in the long run that she was that way, but younger people in general think about privacy differently. There was a period of time where Facebook was trying to say that people of a certain young age didn't care about privacy at all. And I was shocked by that. I thought, "Well it's not that they don't care. It's that they don't understand that it's important yet". And I think as Gen Z got older they care about privacy a lot more than we expected them to. And now I think I'm intrigued by Generation Alpha. Because it seems to me that they might be pulling back and being more offline. Whatever the way it goes, it's going to be in line with the technology available.

I say this because smartphones changed absolutely everything when they came along. The fact that you can have the entire internet, everyone in your life, everything in your life all contained in a device that you carry around everywhere. Like that's not going away, it's a permanent part of people's lives. There is no longer a digital second life, your "first life" is digital. For Gen Z and younger people there are some serious challenges they had to overcome with technology and their own life as they grew up, so I try to learn from them. They have different attitudes towards this kind of thing.

Ioana-Iulia Cazacu: Following on from that is going to be a big question because we very nicely went down this discussion about the audience. I was wondering what your methodology is when aiming to define an audience. How do you tease out characteristics about the audience and create a profile that can be used by developers?

Jen Bolton: Well, it's easier if you have a game already out. But, if you're at the concept stage finding out, the basics like the demographic information always give you a decent starting place. Then we do market research and look at competitors, and we talk to people in the demographic who play those games. Finding good sources for talking to people is always a challenge. This is where having a game in soft launch helps because you can then talk to your players. But when you don't have that, you have to pick the best match for the people that you think are going to be your players.

For us at Mojiworks it was more than just about the game because when you're on a social platform, you're not there to play games necessarily, you're there for the people. So the game has to fit into the context of the social network and connect you with the people that you care about. So sometimes "your people" are going to be people who are not like you. On Facebook we used to have five personas for this. The most interesting one being we had the persona we named Bob. Bob was like someone's dad who doesn't care about the game at all and will never play but does care about the people. And so if there's a small thing that Bob can do that will help someone else to keep playing he would do it. My thinking was that he could somehow still play an important role if given the right tools even if he didn't care for playing. Understanding the type of relationships between players is the kind of social research I find totally fascinating. And this stuff it's not so platform-specific, and having access to talk to our players on different platforms helped us shape this player map.

Obviously we have done this for every platform we worked on: Facebook, Snapchat and Discord. Every time we've gotten a little bit better and found out even more. The picture of the audience and their relationships have been a little bit clearer. In our case the platforms can help a ton too. Discord had a clear vision for their audience and their behaviours. From there we are always doing additional research to understand more and to validate what we get told. But across platforms we're seeing a lot of the similar stuff even if the demographics are different, no matter the age and how they manifested interhuman relationships are similar. And a lot of that is about asking the right questions.

Ioana-Iulia Cazacu: Our audience is predominantly Gen Z, and they are said to be very open and opinionated. Is that what you found?

Jen Bolton: Yes, they also like just having conversations with you. If they can tell there was a human behind the account they are curious about who that is, but even when they didn't know anything about us, they would chat with us like we were one of their friends, asking how we are doing, telling us their problems or even ask us life questions. This is a very good position to be in as a researcher where people want to organically engage with you on that level.

But obviously we are not just chatting about random subjects with the players. There is always a hypothesis that you're trying to test or question. So we frequently aim to ask them questions about the game in these channels especially if they warmed up to us and they are open to tell us more. We don't just talk in text with them either. We organise play sessions and with their permission we record them as they interact with us and each other. This is because as the interviewer or the researcher, you want to focus fully on the people and the moment and you need to actively listen to what they're saying. So recording things, whether it's to get a transcript in text or just record a video to be able to reference a specific instance that happened in a playtest is great. It also leaves us free to think about the user and what they're actually saying.

This is the huge advantage with a direct platform and access to the community that plays your games because you get to see people in their own environment, you get to listen to them about how they like to play the game and with who. It creates a clearer, more sympathetic view of your audience.

Ioana-Iulia Cazacu: So you have spent a lot of time being a liaison between the audience and the dev team, I was wondering if you could tell us more about increasing customer empathy for the team while they are working on a live game that has a lot of feedback?

Jen Bolton: There are two sides to that really. First bit is about connecting with the players in the first place, opening that conversation and allowing them to tell me and by extension us, what they really care about. Making sure we do that well with empathy towards the user, their feelings, and their needs. Second bit is about helping the team understand what is the emotional intention of what's being communicated and what it ultimately means.

So we analyse what we're being told from individual users. We synthesise it into a pool of understanding we can use in a more general sense. This is how we construct the different types of users (personas). We aim not only to communicate that stuff clearly but also want to make the dev team feel things like the audience does. Because as a researcher and liaison I get to feel that with players, and I want to pass it on. The collaboration between player insights and development has revolved around making use of storytelling to convey player emotion. This is meant to help the dev team understand better who they are addressing when working through different problems or features. We also give everyone on the team access to the community; they can go on our Discord server and see what goes on there. They get a sense of the different personalities, and they get a sense of what people are asking us.

We use a lot of product psychology, and I specifically did a course for this that really helped us not only craft the player story for the team but understand the player's story more deeply ourselves. In this course they talk a lot about the emotional user journey of the player through the "app" in their case, and shifting the focus from what happens to the player to how the player feels is a huge deal for us and the dev team. At the end of the day the dev team needs to solve whatever it is that people are talking about, and understanding the full story is crucial for empathy.

Ioana-Iulia Cazacu: Empathy is the very base of a customer-led approach and its usefulness goes beyond just having to work on a live game. I think recently because the games are such a big time and money investment they tend to be less authorial and more of a collaboration between makers and users. The actual boxed game doesn't quite exist in the same way anymore. Pretty much everyone uses testing, soft launches, LiveOps and updates; ultimately you want to give your game the best chance at being loved by people.

Jen Bolton: You are right, and the whole reason I started doing what I do now was because I wanted to help people to enhance their relationships through games, and that required dialogue with the people using it. I do not believe that quality time can only be spent face to face anymore. Sure, there are things that you cannot do online, things like hugging someone, you can yet have a sense of their full presence in a room. It's all different, but emotional connection is still very much possible. And we are seeing the effects now that time has passed since the internet became a thing. There are plenty of people like myself that have made lifelong relationships online. And we see this in the interviews as well. People are telling us that they play with their online friends. Many of them met through Discord in private smaller servers and they have very high-quality relationships with each other. They use games as a vehicle or a playground for interacting. So having a game that they all feel comfortable playing is important, mostly something that isn't hugely skill-based. This gives them more room to focus on the people that they're playing with. Of course different people have different preferences in games, but in general we see that games with a lower cognitive demand do better for mixed groups and social play.

Ioana-Iulia Cazacu: It's fascinating. I guess there is much about this audience that you learn through all these interviews and observing them over the years. What would you say it's the most surprising thing about them?

Jen Bolton: I was surprised with how much ease research participants interacted one-on-one with us, especially on a platform like Snapchat. I had so many conversations that weren't necessarily about the game but about people's lives or them wanting advice or just to vent to someone. Maybe it's in the nature of the medium because these games are embedded in social platforms. But I was surprised by the volume of that for sure.

I was also a little bit surprised by the number of people who would ask us to help them to just make new friends and wanting to expand their social circles. It was interesting because at the time we were under the impression people were using these places only for real-life friends. But what we are seeing is actually people wanting to expand their real-life circle. It is about true friends in the sense that they don't want to play with strangers, but that does not mean they don't want to meet new people.

Plenty of things will surprise you when you do this kind of work. You'll always see people in communities that behave the opposite way to what you expect. And there are always outliers as well. You have to separate one from the other, distil what is most relevant and that can be challenging sometimes with qualitative research because of the smaller sample sizes.

I don't exactly know when the shift happened from "it's weird to meet people online" to "that's what we all kinda do". I am talking generally as well, not just about games. The pandemic however really solidified the "normalcy" of it because it forced it all on people. I don't think we are even gonna fully go back. I mentioned I met my husband online, and no one now thinks that it's strange. And I can feel a bit smug about it because I feel like I understood this all along. COVID highlighted the need for social contact when all we could do was go online and I think a lot of people realised that actually it can be quite effective: you can keep existing bonds alive but you can also make new ones. If some people were sceptical before, they cannot deny it now.

Ioana-Iulia Cazacu: The pandemic was both an accelerant but also just something that coincided I believe with the late adoption stage for social media. I'm curious to see where that's going in the future because the next generation has grown up with these blurred lines between virtual and real-life identity and building friendships anywhere. It is just the way things are now.

Jen Bolton: It is possible doing things in real life will feel more novel and that people will treat hanging out in person the way they treated hanging out online. I think online gives you more opportunity to develop a habit with people and have things sort of a tradition. Gen Alpha will have a different view about what the "normal" proposition between spending time with people in real life versus online is. That is of course not to say they will not spend time with each other in person. It just feels like that will be more of an event and online hanging out is the new standard.

I think trends will always ebb and flow. People doing things because while it feels novel and then drop it off again. Fundamentally Gen Alpha will have the internet fundamentally embedded in their experience of the world and that's going to make them think in a more fluid way about this all. I'm sure there'll always be emerging platforms and you know new things to learn online. But the more used you are with the internet, the more you understand that this is the state of the online space in general. I think more so than the older generation, probably those accustomed to the internet understand that this space is something you must keep up with.

Ioana-Iulia Cazacu: I am very sad to see this interview come to a close, but I was wondering if you had any last nuggets of wisdom that you think are fundamental to share.

Jen Bolton: I'd say that ultimately it's all about empathy and listening. As making the people you talk to feel comfortable, get in their shoes, understand their feelings and their needs. And for the stuff we do that approach should not be too formal because we are talking to people about the games they play. There is emotion there we need to understand. It's about building that kind of rapport with your players, which is a really important skill and something to look for in community managers and user researchers alike.

It's also important to understand what people (the audience) get out of talking to you (the developer) in the first place because they do this for a reason. So how can we as a people who care give them more of what they want when they talk to us? It's important people feel seen and listened to and the other side of this is of course fighting on behalf of the audience for the most common problems to be solved.

Another more practical tip is writing down before a series of user tests what you expect to find. This is so I can get all of my own assumptions out of my mind. If I got these assumptions on paper I am not worried about losing the ideas and it helps me stay curious and really listen to the things the people are saying. I also try to never assume what people mean. When they use certain phrases or words, I prefer asking for clarification. This way you can make people like to feel understood and you get your own personal perspective into the results. Always ask questions, as many as you can, and go with where the natural conversation takes you.

Last but not least is creating excellent working relationships with your team and collaborating closely on not just the detail of day-to-day feature work, but on all the fun emotional work. Include them as co-owners of the process and access to understanding their audience. It is important that the team understands the players not only rationally but also emotionally.

Ioana-Iulia Cazacu: That was a great way to conclude the interview and thank you so much for sharing your thoughts on the topic. It was a fascinating discussion, and I hope the readers will enjoy it as much as I did.

chapter 7

The hyper-social audience

We coined the term "hyper-social games" at Mojiworks around 2019, a couple of years into developing social games for Facebook Messenger. By that point we knew as a team the kind of social games we were making on these platforms, and the differences between what we were doing and the earlier Facebook games were so significant we thought they needed their own name. We more or less stumbled upon the term "hyper-social" when hyper-casual games were starting to ramp up in the mobile market.

Contrary to what the term "hyper-social" might suggest at first glance, this genre is not a mix of hyper-casual and social games; in fact, they have little to do with hyper-casual games in many ways. Instead it uses the same word etymology; "hyper-" means "above normal" or "going beyond". In the case of hyper-causual games this meant that they were extremely casual; the whole core revolved around these incredibly simple mechanics. That being said we took the prefix "hyper-" and added it to social games because that is what we think these games are: they are the version that takes the idea of a social game and runs with it, going beyond what we have seen before.

The main reason why we thought these games needed a new term to describe them was not only to do with their much improved social capabilities but also to do with their presence on platforms that look incredibly different to each other yet can still be considered social spaces. The term "social game" described very much a snapshot in time, predominantly referring to games on Facebook but in general referring to games hosted on a social media platform. In turn, "hyper-social" is meant to be broader, and it encompasses games whose main goal is socialising on platforms that allow the user to do so with ease, be they strictly considered "social media platforms" or not.

The breakthrough in understanding what hyper-social games were really about was when we started to understand more about the audience these games were being played by. In strictly demographic terms we saw that games on these platforms are predominantly played by younger Millennials, Gen Z and even younger with a gender split of around 50/50 (varying slightly between platforms). However, the most important thing about this audience is not so much the demographic information but the way they use the internet and consume content.

DOI: 10.1201/9781003314325-10

A lot of trends that have been first noticed among Gen Z specifically spread to encompass the rest of the internet, and those who are involved online have sort of assimilated behaviour via interaction. Currently, Gen Z is the youngest generation with spending power, as a lot of them have come into adulthood in their past few years, and a lot of platforms have seen the opportunity to cater to this generation making them the new "cool place to be".

With all that being said hyper-social games are not about Gen Z specifically or even for them in that way. They are instead for a new generation of players who have a more sophisticated behaviour around their social life online, a group of people who are used to using online as a tool for socialising and self-expression in a way that wasn't previously done. In order to truly understand what kind of people we are addressing, I thought it important to highlight the main traits of the audience I am speaking of.

Online as second nature

Most of this audience grew up with smartphones and the internet at their fingertips, and even those who did not assimilated to the online culture to the point where they cannot really comprehend life without it. Of course access to the World Wide Web is easier than it's ever been and a lot of people have embraced being online and incorporated it into their day-to-day lives to different degrees, but the audience we are talking about is more engrossed than just the surface utility of it. We are talking about people who spend a significant amount of time on the internet; they get all of their information online and use a lot of different social media apps. Each of these social media platforms has different "personas", different friend groups and different conversations. They are very aware of internet culture, they can understand the multiple levels of abstractions that go into understanding a meme and they might even be described by others or even themselves as "chronically online".

Because of this characteristic, this audience presents some unique challenges in the quest to design a game that captures their attention. Firstly, the content must grip them right away; the game is screaming for attention to the mountains of content they have access to so it needs to convince them of its value fast. This is because in a world full of content and information we can only offer so much of our time and emotional energy to a product based on our preconceived value of interacting with that product. When we are talking about games, the perceived value to the player is less tangible than in the case of an app that helps you solve a certain issue they are having. Instead the baseline value of a game revolves around how much "fun" the player expects to be having while playing the game.

The involvement meter

In order to easier visualise the concept of a player starting a game with an initial emotional buy-in, I like to use something I call the "involvement meter". The involvement meter as a concept revolves around the idea that even before we open a game for the first time there is a certain degree of energy we are "prepared" to expend to engage with it to see if it meets our expectations and delivers on its value proposition. There is a multitude of factors that determine how a user might feel about a game initially and how high that involvement meter starts for the player. The most important of those factors are:

- Has the user spent time/money to get the game and if so how much?
- Did they get any recommendation for the game either from a friend or another trusted source like a streamer they follow?
- Are they going to join their friends in the game and play together?
- Is the game part of a franchise they have played before and, if so, how much "franchise loyalty" do they have for it?
- Have they previously seen content online as proof of value?
- Is the game positioning itself as a genre the user enjoys?
- Does it form any associations with any older titles that the user might find nostalgic value in?
- What is the saturation of the market at this specific moment?
- What is the person's overall appetite for playing games in general?

Because of these factors, the player comes to the game with a certain amount of energy ready to expend in order to find out if the game will suit their tastes and satisfy their desires for entertainment. The amount of involvement in the meter naturally reduces over time unless the player is given something satisfactory that bumps up the involvement. Similarly, if the user is frustrated or dissatisfied with an aspect of the game, involvement takes a hit decreasing in a larger increment. When the involvement reaches zero, the player decides that the game is not for them and leaves the game potentially never to return, unless other means outside the game brings their involvement back up.

There are many factors that can lower involvement and the amount it decreases has to do with how fundamentally the issue contradicts the expectations of the player. I like to split these into two main categories: fundamental misalignments and secondary misalignments.

Fundamental misalignments are the things that directly contradict the expectations the player had in mind and as a result the dip in involvement is sudden and significant. Such factors can be:

- The game far surpasses the player's ability to engage, be it because of accessibility reasons or difficulty reasons.
- The game presents views and topics in opposition to the player's strongly held views.
- The player is fundamentally disappointed in the quality of the product.
- The game is dependent on the player interacting with monetisation tactics that they are not happy to interact with.

Secondary misalignments are the things that bother the player but do not necessarily contradict the core of their expectations such as:

- The game holds gratification away from the player for too long.
- The game feels unrewarding or unsatisfying to play.
- The player gets confused by the game content.
- The game pushes mechanics the player doesn't enjoy.
- The player feels treated unfairly by the game.

The involvement meter is a useful tool for the designer as a way of mapping the experience, especially when analysing a game experience retroactively with data at hand to compare. It allows us to dissect why users might be dropping off at a certain point, allowing us to see their point of view and embrace compassionate solutions.

However, for casual games especially, the involvement meter is useful in understanding the experience in the first session. This is because free-to-play casual games require less involvement on the player's behalf, the player invested nothing and they only aim to interact with the game casually. This means that the first user experience has to be tailored to grab their attention and encourage them to keep exploring the game and find value in it (Figure 7.1).

I have noticed there is a sort of distaste or frustration with this on the part of some developers, regarding the lower initial (and maybe overall) involvement of more casual gamers, sometimes to a degree that makes them see these people as less than because of their commitment. I believe however that there is little use in lamenting the differences in initial user engagement between the different audiences and platforms as it does not tell us anything about how to better design for them. Ultimately casual gamers will never be hardcore gamers. For one reason or another that is not something they enjoy or want to engage with, so invalidating the way they like to enjoy these games serves no one. Every audience has things that make them tick, things that get them excited about interacting with a product, and the way to make something they love is to cater to those things as best we can.

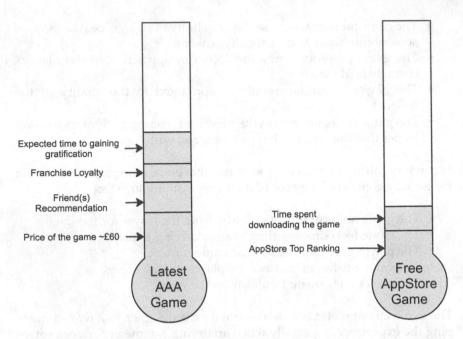

Figure 7.1 Example of initial involvement meters for two different types of games

Masters of online non-verbal communication

The concept of non-verbal communication in the field of social science began in the 1950s and 1960s with the works of Ray L. Birdwhistell and Edward T. Hall. This type of communication refers to the ability of one person to conjure a concept in someone else's mind using only non-verbal ways of interaction (not using words spoken or written). As mentioned in Chapter 3, however, a lot of these other means of communication that people are so incredibly used to using in their real-world conversations every day are limited or do not exist in the same way when communicating online with someone. This is why the internet evolved with time to include new ways of incorporating meaning into something inferred from the context of the conversation.

Face-to-face non-verbal communication is often divided into four different categories:

- **Kinesics**: The array of actions that are usually referred to under the umbrella of "body language". This includes facial expressions, eye contact, touch and other gestures.
- **Proxemics**: The use of space in the conversation, and how people use the environment in order to communicate with each other. This includes things like proximity or the position in relation to other objects.

- **Paralanguage**: Other vocal qualities and sounds that are not words. This includes things like the tone of voice and other sounds that communicate emotion such as laughter.
- **Chronemics**: The time component of a conversation and how that time is used during the course of a conversation. This includes how we allot time to different conversation topics and the frequency of back-and-forth conversation.

By exploring the topic of non-verbal communication and analysing the internet and especially the very internet-savvy audience we spoke of, I realised that for all of these different types there exists some kind of digital equivalent. Of course the difference here is that understanding physical non-verbal communication comes naturally to most of us because they have been around for as long as the human race, however, online non-verbal communication devices are not only very new (invented within the people's lifetimes) but they also have a subtlety that requires persistent if not total immersion in the online world to fully understand.

Unlike the real world, I believe the lines between these different types of non-verbal conversation to be more blurred, as there is no real "body" to speak of when communicating over social media or a chat app. Although they might identify with their "user profile" and that user is "located" somewhere on the internet, the expression is not quite the same. Keep this in mind as we continue dissecting the parallels between the classic styles of non-verbal communication in real life and their digital counterparts.

Kinesics

Common facsimiles of human facial expressions are emoji and other animated versions of a digital avatar aiming to reproduce facial expressions. Although, as mentioned in previous chapters, an emoji can be used in a sincere or ironic way, that context is derived from other means of non-verbal communication much like we do in real life (for example when a person smiles but we know they are being ironic from the context of the conversation). Similarly, gifs or images are also used often to express emotion.

But emoji and the other media used do not limit themselves to depicting emotions through the depiction of a human emoting. There are plenty of emoji depicting objects and even complex concepts, and the gallery of videos, images and gifs is practically endless. When the media we share portrays a person emoting in one way or another, the parallel with kinesics is clear to draw. But what happens when, for example, the media in question is portraying an inanimate object? The beauty of the internet is that we are not limited to our physical body to express emotion or to give more context to something. This means we can expand to include "feelings" as embodied by other things. We do this by emotionally interpreting this ourselves and then sending it to the other person as a representation of our own feelings and as additional context to our digital verbal conversation.

Proxemics

In the digital world, the closest parallel to draw with the positioning in a space of two people's communication is the place the two are communicating in. Different platforms facilitate different kinds of conversation and the sharing of different content, therefore much can be derived from the location of such a conversation. Are we communicating in a one-to-one private chat or are we using a group chat? Are we using a platform like Snapchat in order for our conversation to be quick and ephemeral or are we using a platform like Discord that keeps all conversations and allows us to have multiple channels with the same people on different topics? Users will build different personas for the different places they are in, and they might, depending on who they are with and where the conversation is taking place, infer more detail from the conversation.

Location on the internet is a nebulous concept. Although we can define it by the platform hosting or the people involved, there is no concept of physical proximity in the social virtual space. Even when we are talking about communication over video call the proximity to the camera does not encompass the same expressive value because the joint space we are in is the virtual one, not the physical one in which a person is moving.

Paralanguage

The audio aspect of non-verbal communication is probably the least emulated in the online space. The closest approximation to it would be the propagation of sound bites over TikTok. Technically, this is not entirely non-verbal because many of these clips contain verbal components, but I would argue that the meaning of these sound bites becomes abstracted over time to a point where they come to carry different or additional meaning to the original content. Because of this reason I would suggest that the repeated use of sound bites on different types of videos that are not the original becomes with time a form of non-verbal communication where the receiver of the information no longer listens to the content and instead derives additional context from it to apply to whatever the video footage associated with it is.

Another way of looking at this is to explore what other methods of online non-verbal communication serve the same purpose as paralanguage in real-life conversation. Tone is notoriously difficult to infer from written conversation. This is when emoji can come into play again and be used as additional context for the tone of a message.

Chronemics

The time component remains fairly immutable across digital and non-digital communication, although sometimes time seems to pass differently when it comes to online communication. When we are talking about text asynchronous communication over the internet there are different expectations of the user given on the platform of communication. Similarly, some platforms might display additional temporal information about the user such as "online a few minutes ago", which may affect the context of a late reply.

Non-verbal communication and games

But why are the styles of non-verbal communication important to look at in the context of games and especially in the context of games with a social component? Here are a few reasons why I believe it is very important to explore this topic.

Firstly, this is now the language of the internet. All these different ways of communicating are making communication online more vibrant and more expressive. The audience we are discussing is very versed in this language. They know the ins and outs of it and they use it out of habit without thinking of it, much like we use physical non-verbal communication. Analysing how they interact online and the kind of tools they have embraced in order to be more expressive tells us a lot about the kind of things we can do with social games to allow them to feel a truer connection with each other.

Secondly, I believe there is something to be said about the complexity of what could be classified as "non-verbal" communication online because while I believe equating it to real life does shed an interesting light on the more basic facts of this type of communication online, it is not enough to define it. For example, how do artefacts like memes or game shares fit into this? Even if they have a verbal component, that verbal communication does not come from the player and it is rather a reflection of their presence online, so can it then be considered a type of "non-verbal" communication?

We found that the audience we are looking at loves communicating with each other in all these little ways the language of shareable content can take. In the case of a social game, we can curate the game to create shareable content that allows the player more freedom of expression revolving around what they do inside the game.

If we would like to cater the experience of shareable content and make the player truly want to share using the patterns of their other communications online becomes very telling. This often means that we as developers must not only speak to our audience and try to understand how these new methods of communication are being used, but we have to immerse ourselves in it and try to experience it for ourselves. It is part of research as much as playing another game for inspiration.

Virtual gift givers

The act of giving is one that has fascinated anthropologists for a very long time. The reasons people give gifts to each other and how they treat the act of giving and receiving varies from culture to culture, but the purpose of it is always social, even if it is more transactional than sentimental. In principle, the different types of gift-giving can have one of the following purposes: communication, social exchange, economic exchange and socialisation (Sherry Jr., 1983). This theory of gift-giving is constructed based on the exchange of physical gifts but does not only refer to things that have economic value. After all, the gift of a thoughtful note is worth more than the paper it's written on. The true value of a gift is derived from many components that go beyond their actual physical value and incorporate the nature and closeness of the relationship between the giver and receiver, the intention of the gift, the purpose of the item and the frequency of the act of gifting. Because of this, it's very interesting to look into the subject of gifting from a digital perspective, where the "item" being sent is virtual.

The comparison between "real" and virtual gifts is not one-to-one, as there is an additional facet to be considered and that is the perceived ephemerality of the virtual item. Object permanence dictates that an object does not cease to exist when we are not looking at it; its existence is not linked to our perception of it. But could we say the same for digital items? In theory, the answer is yes. If one owns a sword in a game, said sword does not disappear once we turn the game off. Data is stored either remotely in a server or locally on the device to ensure that ownership of the item stays with the owner. However, the nature of the medium itself feels transitory. The existence of that object is entirely reliant on the running of the game servers by the makers of the game and/or the existence of data that associates the owner with the owned item.

Virtual items are also not always devoid of economic value. The most obvious example is that of items that can be gifted that are purchased with real-life currency (e.g. character skins in a multiplayer online battle arena [MOBA]), but the users accept the transitory nature of their investment upon purchase. Recently, there have been movements to create digital items that hold some irrefutable value in the form of NFTs (non-fungible tokens), but those items too rely on the existence of the economic infrastructure that created them in order to hold their value because there is no physical component we can apply object permanence to.

That is not to say that virtual gift-giving has no value, just that it operates under different parameters and in fact the audience we are talking about has ascribed a lot of meaning to gift-giving in the online space, as a lot of their communication happens in this medium. This is why it's worth analysing what said gift means to both the giver and the receiver.

The pure virtual gift

The concept of the pure gift is disputed in anthropology, the idea being that in order for the gift to be "free" or "pure" it must not create any kind of social obligation between the giver and the receiver. It is argued that in order for such a gift to exist three different conditions must be met:

1. There is no reciprocity.
2. The receiver doesn't perceive the gift as a gift.
3. The giver doesn't perceive the gift as a gift.

Anthropologists then argue that such a "gift" therefore does not exist, and there are multiple conversations as to how and why that would be.[1] However, when exploring online social relationships and communication, I would argue the "free" gift has more of a fighting chance at existing because of the aforementioned perceived lack of permanence.

As we have also established, gift-giving can serve the purpose of communication. With that in mind, we can then analyse the online phenomenon of sharing content first in a more general sense and then in a more pointed sense as it pertains to sharing in social games. As discussed throughout this chapter, the number one way to create a game that helps players socialise is to understand how socialisation and communication happen online. While we can see the use of memes, gifs and videos as a way of online non-verbal communication, we can see them also as a gift depending on the context of the conversation. Sometimes the sharing of content does not happen as a response to a conversation but rather as a gesture of recognition between the sender and the receiver. Sharing content online can be the virtual equivalent of a gift accompanied by the phrase " I saw this and I thought of you". Analysing this kind of "gift-giving" where there are no real items being exchanged but content is, we can see that there is no expected reciprocity. The receiver does not really receive it as a gift and the sender does not consider it to be one. It does therefore fulfil all the criteria of a free gift. So can it be considered a gift at all? I would argue yes, because the exchange of content in this way, while it has no monetary value or physical component, can still be seen as the sending of an "item" from one person to the other. Furthermore, it fulfils two of the main purposes of gift-giving: communication and socialisation. The perceived value of the item on the receiver's end is derived from the interpretation of the sender and its association with what the receiver likes to engage with or is in other ways interested in.

The same type of mentality applies to content that is created or generated inside the game but has the same trait of being more generally relatable. The purpose of the share here is entirely social in nature, meaning that the person sending the "item" does not intend to establish any in-game mechanical connection but instead they shared as "proof of relationship".

In-game gifts

In-game gifting mechanics can be more closely analysed under the framework of real-life gift-giving, as most commonly there is a specific digital artefact associated with it, be it permanent or temporary. This lends the gift a mechanical purpose within the framework of the game (i.e. the receiver can "use" what they have received as a gift to in some way to enhance their experience of the game). Players have different mechanical motivations for offering digital gifts in a game:

- **To ease someone's experience with the game**: This can take the form of giving a more powerful item to a lower-level friend to help them have an easier time.
- **To enhance collaboration and social gameplay**: This can take the form of offering someone an item that is purposefully there to help teamwork.
- **To help them establish a certain status**: This can take the form of coveted items or commendations.
- **To help them avoid spending real-life currency**: This can take the form of sending someone more "energy" or "hearts" in a game in order to continue playing.
- **To establish group uniformity**: This can take the form of specific looks or loadouts for the members of the group that establish them externally as a team.

For all of the aforementioned mechanical reasons, the emotional reasons for people to offer gifts are the same as in real-life gift-giving: expressing companionship, marking an event/upholding gift-giving tradition, expressing gratitude and expressing guilt or regret. Most commonly, when we are talking about video games and gift-giving in this context we are seeing "expressing companionship" as a more prominent motivator for people to give, but other emotional motivations pop up from time to time as well.

The audience we are looking at fosters a lot of complex long-term online connections. This phenomenon is of course not entirely new, as this kind of behaviour could be observed back in the 1990s and early 2000s, but it has become a lot more commonplace than it used to be. A lot of these relationships might be entirely online, with the people involved being in different countries, making traditional gift-giving a lot more difficult. For these reasons and for the ease and convenience of this type of gift, players of this audience are quite enthusiastic at the opportunity to send someone a virtual present.

The creative community

The audience we are referring to are not passive consumers of entertainment; they love being involved and getting creative, and they are informed and willing to contribute. There is an argument to be made that the way we create products in general can be approached differently when relying on user-created content as a valuable source of information about our audience (Rathore et al., 2016). The users we are designing for are not only very comfortable with content creation online, but they are also using it as a way of expressing their ideas directly, making it a gold mine of uncensored ideas and emotions that can tell the true story of the product we are trying to create.

The concept of social co-creation (Rathore et al., 2016) describes a product design approach where the user is no longer a passive receiver of content but instead contributes to the making of said product by taking an active part in the development process. This means that development is no longer one-sided and instead becomes more of a dialogue between the makers and the audience. Social media is a treasure trove of content made by the audience for others like them, which is an incredibly valuable resource for a game regardless of whether you are making a social game or not. It is undeniable that social media is more than a platform for marketing and visibility, and active involvement of the developers with the people on social media leads to fostering a community of individuals that as a group can offer true insights on what the audience desires. But this desire to create content does not stop at the border of social media; it extends into the game and creates a link between the virtual world of the game and the virtual world of the social media platform.

When we are discussing content creation in the context of a socially connected game, there are three types that we can consider:

1. **Content about the game posted independently to social media**: This content is created by the user entirely on their own (i.e. not using a bespoke feature from the game to capture and share). This may include content from the game such as video captures of screenshots, but it may also take the form of fan art, fanfiction and opinion pieces.

2. **Content about the game shared from inside the game**: This refers specifically to content created inside the game and shared via the means of sharing mechanics as described in Chapter 6. The main difference between this type of content and the previous is the freedom with which the player can express their creativity. While independently shared content is more free-form and creative, it also takes more effort to create and post.
3. **Content that is meant to be shared and interacted with inside the game**: This refers to content that is destined to be consumed inside the game as part of the content, most commonly using developer-made tools to do so such as player-made maps, game mods or other game content created by the audience.

These different types of content creation appeal to different users, depending on their skills and ability to create content, as well as the ultimate goal of sharing the content made with others. The players will engage with ways of creating content that are appropriate for their levels of involvement in the game (remember the earlier explained involvement meter). A low-engagement player might use an in-game way to share content but will not create fan art or even tweet about a game. In contrast, high-involvement players will engage with more labour-intensive content creation partly driven by their own interests but also with a desire to express their ideas and opinions publicly about the game towards the community.

In special cases, such as famous online creators, the creation and sharing of content becomes a product in itself to be consumed. This edge case, while interesting in its own right, does not really reflect the general audience's attitude towards content creation, as it is heavily influenced by platform content trends, monetary incentives and their own audience demands.

The tools available and the commonality of content creation make the members of this audience very expressive in this way. This means that not only do they have ideas, but they love getting involved with games in these different ways. Especially in the context of user-generated content inside the game, we have seen that players really enjoyed contributing their ideas to improve the game, even when we talk about casual players. In the trivia game we published on Snap Games, we aimed to offer players an easy tool to submit questions. This is because we realised that what our audience craved most was currently relevant questions that could not be done by adding packs of verified questions to the game because they would be obsolete before we could even add them. Approximately 6% of the users became content creators for the game, most of them being very dedicated to submitting quality questions on a number of different subject matters. In order to make sure the content was accurate, we had to have an internal system for approving questions as well as screening for questions that were not appropriate. If a question was wrong or out of date, players could also notify us through the game, which made them the masters of their own content. This collaborative process resulted in content that was more relevant to the audience.

Overall, the willingness and ability of this audience to create more suitable content are incredibly powerful and something to be considered when possible. Even when the game itself cannot offer the players the ability to submit their creations to the game, embracing content creation as something that will happen and fostering it as much as possible is vital. A game should do this by offering players tools that eliminate friction in creating such content for a greater feeling of self-expression, but they should also read into the content created about the game in order to foster that process of social co-creation.

Note

1. For more details on the concept of a "free" gift, I encourage you to read Soumhya Venkatesan's article in the *Journal of the American Ethnological Society*, 138(1), 47–57, 2011 titled "The Social Life of a 'Free' Gift", which is a good synopsis of previous research on the topic.

chapter 8

Designing for a social-centric audience

Experimentation is vital when working in a new sector of games. Each platform is used differently and attracts a different type of user. Social media games are even more affected by the platform they are on because of their close integration with the platform hosting them and the multipurpose nature of these platforms. On a social platform, games must not only surface on top of any of the other social activities that they have to do, but they also have to integrate fully with the features and quirks of the platform that the users expect. So even though social games are technically separate from the platform they are on, the users do not treat them as such mostly because the purpose of them coming to the platform is socialising and not playing. And although a game might be the perfect tool for socialising, it's always considered in the greater context of the app itself. For all of these reasons, designing social games presents a very specific audience challenge where one must first understand the way users are already using their base platform (social media) and then apply that to the way the game is being played, as we spoke about in the last chapter. This means that in order to captivate a wide audience and really engross users we must design through the lens of this different platform, often creating bespoke games that would not "work" outside of these social platforms or even on other similar platforms. Even if we think back to the early days of social games on Facebook, we realise that porting a game to a platform is not enough to make it reach the full audience. Instead it is about understanding the behaviour of the audience on that platform and making use of features to fully integrate a game in the day-to-day use of it. Utilising these features does more than help propagate the game to a larger audience, it also ensures that the game can reach its full social potential and thus serve the primary purpose of the people coming to a social app. The presence of a game on a social platform is definitely not enough to justify calling it a "social" game in my opinion, and it is instead about making the purpose of socialising its primary use case. That means that all game design decisions must be taken from the lens of what is beneficial socially even when the decision contradicts conventional game design logic.

DOI: 10.1201/9781003314325-11

When designing a video game we tend to consider things like difficulty curves, rewards or daily reengagement. These are all important things that make a game great. But from my personal experience building a game that involves other people has an additional layer of social complexity that needs to always be considered no matter what we are talking about. This however does not mean that everything about these games has to be a shared experience but rather that at any point in the loop the shared experience is considered. The balance between personal and group mechanics and activities must be such that it allows the player to identify with the contents of the game both individually and as a group, and establish that connection we spoke of in Chapter 2.

What the team and I noticed throughout developing these kinds of games is that certain social mechanics are not universally applicable, meaning that different demographics and platforms have preferences for certain kinds of social mechanics. As I have mentioned throughout this book, the social platform itself tends to set the tone for the kind of social interaction that is possible in the games that inhabit them. Directly researching the audience and their response to these different social features inside the game is still very important. While platform features are directly meant to serve the audience we are addressing, there is no telling why a choice was made. Ideally there will also be close communication between the hosting platforms and the games in order to build social features that enhance the game experience that might not have cropped up otherwise.

This whole process must always be guided by a healthy dose of trial and error because there is nothing quite as complex as human beings and understanding the way they socialise. There is no simulation that can be run to approximate how people will use a product, especially when the product in question is primarily made to facilitate human interaction. With that being said there are things we learned about the social audience we speak of and while these thoughts originate here for a specific reason there is definitely overlap with designs for games with a social purpose on other platforms.

Design around their lives

It's a false assumption that games are only in competition with other games for the player's time and attention. In reality, games are in "competition" with everything else that can happen in a player's life, such as other recreational activities, personal obligations and work.

There are a couple of ways that we can create something the player will choose to engage with. Although they seem quite opposite to each other, a good balance of the two can create a game that is both compelling and respectful.

1. Using design to captivate the player's attention and make them want to play the game to the exclusion of other activities they could be doing. For example, being completely immersed in the world of a game so that the player loses track of time.
2. Using a product-led approach to understand the market and design the use of a game around the kind of resources your audience has. For example, designing something that is meant to be played on the commute home because the audience is young professionals with busy lives.

Compelling the player to get absorbed by the game can be a force for good. After all, many of us remember playing a game for hours and forgetting about the world around us, and to some degree escapism is part of the charm of games. When we design to captivate our audience we will inevitably want to make it so the player puts down the game already thinking about the next time they are going to pick it back up. This can however become exploitative when the game is employing psychological tricks to push the player to do things they would not do of their own accord. Employing exploitative tactics can happen by accident when the designer is so focused on encouraging play that they end up creating something which has a negative impact on the player's quality of life. This is of course true for any type of game regardless of the social component, but the group dynamics create an added layer of danger of manipulation when it comes to games that are meant to be played with other players. Already exploitative mechanics can be amplified by peer pressure or unfair competition. The product-centric approach is there to make sure that playing the game is additive to a person's life rather than all-consuming. Being mindful of who is playing your game, what kind of time and resources they have access to and building a model that works both for the player and for the developer is the way you can build long-term loyalty. We will also discuss the topic of social–ethical design in more detail in Chapter 9.

To be able to build such a model we, as developers, must not only understand our audience and their lives but also understand the impact that different features have on their lives. How does the audience receive a specific feature and how do they use it based on the time and resources they have on hand? The easiest way to think about this is through the diagram in Figure 8.1.

This diagram is simple enough when we are talking about a single-player game, but when we are talking about social and multiplayer games, social relationships make it inherently more complicated. This is because the question is no longer only about what the one player enjoys but what the group enjoys, or even more important what kind of content they like to engage in when they are together. It also becomes about what is affordable

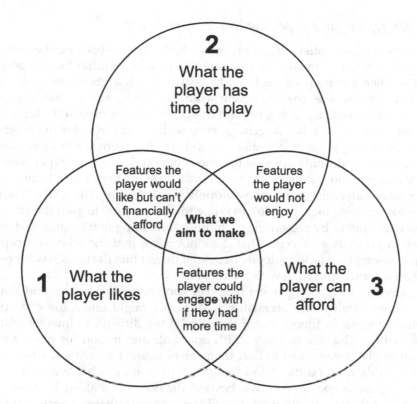

Figure 8.1 Venn diagram of how the player's resources and abilities influence the game mechanics they interact with

for all members of the group and what one deems a reasonable price to pay for a game they might engage with exclusively when being with others. And last but not least it comes to the age-old difficulty of scheduling an activity to enjoy together.

Because of this complexity, designing games that fit all these factors for a group of people can be a bit of a daunting task. This type of complexity can also be a blessing in disguise. In the same way that other people can hinder a player from picking up a game, they can also help convince them to do so when they would otherwise not make that decision for themselves. Just as we discussed in Chapter 1, friends will actually put in significant effort to convince their friends to play a game that they for one enjoy.

So how can we best approach the problem of making a game that can fit into the intersections of those circles for multiple friends in a group? There are a few things to take into consideration and techniques we can apply to give the game a better chance of being adopted by a group.

Making your game appealing to a wide audience

Groups of friends offer a huge advantage to developers because they usually already have similar tastes in entertainment and similar lived experiences. Therefore it's not a big jump to assume that friends are more likely to have similar likes than complete strangers, but there are other things we can do as well. But going beyond that, the way to approach the topic is to make a game that has in general very wide appeal in order to encompass as many people as possible. A good starting point when designing things for a wide audience is to use the common desires and experiences of the target audience you are looking at; humans have more things in common with each other than you might think. Making the goal of your game something most people can relate to is a sure way to gain the attention of the public by presenting them with something that is immediately easy to grasp as a concept. That does not mean that the whole concept must be simple or lacking depth, instead it means that the hook has to create an instant connection with the player.

Once in the game, players have yet another barrier to face and that is approachability and accessibility. A player might enjoy the concept behind a game in theory, but if they find it too difficult to interact with they will not be able to enjoy it. It's not at all uncommon for players to want to play a game just to find themselves pushed away by the lack of accessibility or the difficulty of the game. How approachable and accessible a game is goes in this case beyond the need for making it easier to access for those with different disabilities (although that is a very important topic casual games don't consider enough in my opinion). We all have things that affect our "ability" to play, be it not knowing how to use a specific input device like a controller or even not knowing the language in which the game is made. Obviously it's impossible to make the game accessible to everyone, but when it comes to something like a game meant to be played with others, making it easy to access is crucial. The same goes for approachability; the game must welcome those who want to play it irrespective of their past experiences with games and allow them to enjoy the time with their friends.

Inclusivity is quite fundamental: making sure that everyone regardless of who they are can see themselves as part of the game fantasy. Too often inclusivity is overlooked or thrown in as an afterthought to tick certain boxes, but the truth is that if you want people to enjoy your game together there should be no barriers to them doing so. If we want the players to identify with the game and see themselves in the fantasy, we must make use of all the tools we can feasibly create in order for them to create that self-expression. In games where players communicate and interact with others, the ability for them to present themselves in a way that is socially meaningful to them is very important.

Quality is the last but definitely not least factor and an important point to keep in mind when trying to get your game liked by as many people as possible. Quality can manifest in multiple ways, but oftentimes it is predominantly attention to detail and a strong sense of identity that shines through and gives the player more reasons to engage with the game. While simply made hyper-casual games seem to attract a lot of users, the fleetingness of that interaction is not what we are looking for when trying to make a game that a group of people play for a long time. Therefore the game must be of a high standard of quality and encourage the players to explore and play it for longer periods of time for the pure satisfaction of interacting with it.

Making sure your games fit in your audience's schedule

It's safe to assume that people will try to accommodate their own friends when they are proposing they should play a game together. Oftentimes depending on demographics we see people's schedules align in such a way that play patterns emerge. These patterns can be used to accommodate the player better in their play habits especially as they pertain to social play. Say for example our main demographic is still in school, which means they usually have little time to play during the weekdays so they cannot be expected to play every day especially when we factor in multiplayer. This means that the daily social gameplay would be more async, while the longer-term goals and events can rely on more synchronous gameplay, as players will get enough time to schedule playing.

In general, being flexible about when and how the game is played by people together is the best policy. In order to not compromise on the overall social connection people get out of playing a game with others, we need to mould ourselves to the time we know people are already happy to put into the game and time events so that we can fully offer them at a time when we know players will be able to enjoy them best. For this of course we have to be very aware of how people spend their time in the game and the use cases of the game as it behaves out in the wild, which is a lot easier to do when we have real data coming from the game. However, beyond the finesse of following patterns in the audience's schedule, there are plenty of common sense methods to apply in order to make sure we are time aware and respecting the fact that our audience will prioritise their life events to playing our game.

Something mobile game developers learned quite early on is that bite-size content seems to hit a sweet spot for casual audiences very well. These people who were not traditionally considered gamers found this content easy to fit around their busy lives, proving that whether someone plays video games or not has more to do with time than with an innate dislike for games. This is even more true when we are trying to create an experience where more than one person has to be involved for the game to take place. We discovered early on in our multiplayer social game journey that dropping in and out of the game should be expected, and rather than focusing on trying to force the player to stay longer, we should focus on them having such a great time in the moments they play that they can't wait to come back later. Bite-size content and the flexibility to drop in and out of the game allow the player to fit the game into any time slot they have available because the commitment to starting a game is low. And if the content is bite-size and the players have time to spend in the game, then all they have to do is keep going around the loop multiple times.

Because of traditional PC and console multiplayer games a lot of people think synchronously when we discuss multiplayer, which makes sense provided that the truest social experience is derived from a real-time connection with another person. But flexibility is always more desired, after all, you can have the most amazing synchronous multiplayer in the world but if people cannot find the time to engage with it, it has no value to them. This is where layering async features on top of sync features helps give the player different levels of social interaction to engage in. They allow players to work around each other's schedule and even if they don't actually have a chance to meet in game live they can still feel the sense of connection that comes from playing together. Furthermore mixing sync and async also has an added benefit beyond the time flexibility: it gives players the opportunity to experiment and choose the level of social interaction they are happy to have with someone in this context, in the same way that in real-life people use phone calls and text messages for different intensity of interactions.

Making your game affordable to your audience

The free-to-play model has revolutionised the entire gaming market as a whole, but it has especially changed the face of multiplayer games. Making a game free allows access to a lot of people who may not otherwise be able to engage with it by eliminating one of the biggest barriers to entry: the buy-in. Free-to-play goes hand in hand with device coverage. If you can get your game to be compatible with as many different platforms as possible, you can open up access to as wide of a market as possible. A fantastic example of this is *Genshin Impact* which is not only free to play but it's also available on mobile, PC and console. This made *Genshin* one of the biggest games of 2020. It is also one of the highest grossing games in terms of revenue, proving that free-to-play is actually an incredibly clever way to make something that is accessible to the player but still makes the developers enough money to sustain themselves.

But even if the game cannot be free to play for one reason or another, there are other solutions to making a game accessible to a group of people.

World of Warcraft became popular not in small part because of its subscription-based model: it was a lot easier to convince a friend to join you for the price of a month's subscription than it was for a larger flat rate. Other games such as *Don't Starve Together* offer the person purchasing a secondary copy to gift to a friend because they know the game's appeal relies on people playing together, and players might convince more of their friends to join once they have experienced the multiplayer experience. In general it's good to make the pioneer player's job of recommending the game to a friend as easy as possible and the buy-in price is a huge factor at play.

But making the game financially accessible does not stop at the buy-in price because for free-to-play games the "cost" does not just disappear, it gets distributed inside the game. It then follows that for free-to-play, there must also be further methods to give people access to paid content such as join access, trading and gifting mechanics. This is done to even out access to premium content and give all players a good experience. And while it might sound counterintuitive initially, this works to the game's advantage twofold: on one hand, it gives a taste of the kind of content that can be purchased in your game, so even the most sceptical of players might develop a taste for it. On the other hand, those players who cannot afford to access content are being given selective limited access to the premium content making their experience better and them more likely to keep playing, which in turn makes their friends stick around longer as well.

Layering mechanical complexity

It is very tempting to think that multiplayer games must be everything for everyone. After all, they need to appeal to a lot of different people at the same time in order to convince them to play together. In an attempt to create something that everyone would like we feel a desire to cram as many different experiences in our game as possible, even when they may distract from the core. We do this in hopes that the players will go to their friends and say, "Come play this awesome game, it has everything you could possibly want". But in reality what we end up creating is an experience that is confused about its own identity and this harms the new player, making joining a friend paradoxically more difficult.

In my experience the best thing to do in order to capture a wide multiplayer audience, especially a more casual one (but these observations are not limited to casual games), is to make the core experience exciting but simple to understand right away. This simplicity does not imply that there is no depth to the game or that there are no layers of complexity to be discovered over time. What it does mean is that the core of the game is what really matters and that core is easy to "sell". As a new player coming into the game I am unlikely to care about how interesting the levelling system is or what is the meta around crafting objects. Instead what I would need to understand right away is "how is this fun to play with my friends", and this can be done through a clear core that is enticing and easy to get into.

To achieve this the game must make sure to:

- **Have a generally appealing theme**: This does not mean to make a game lack personality, instead it is about drawing from common human experience of what makes an activity satisfying or desirable. This could be anything from the satisfying effect of completing a task to the excitement of competition; wrap the core theme of the game around something universally applicable.
- **Keep the core simple and easy to engage with**: This means that players old and new can come back to the game and pick it (back) up with ease not having to worry about the complexity that lies under the surface. This ensures that people can have a great time together without engaging with all the game's systems.
- **Reveal systems over time**: While the core of the game must be simple, the game itself needs to have depth in order to hold onto the devoted players. So to achieve this complex systems must be revealed to them over time. This protects the new player from the complexity they might not want to engage with, and it offers the engaged players something to make the game feel new again.
- **Hold on to the game's identity**: This means that while the systems are layered and can be considered separately, they still have to gel with one another thematically and/or systemically so the game feels like a singular cohesive experience.

In the end these are just core rules of design that are not altogether new or unique to social experience, but they play a specific important role in the creation of a game that is aimed at a group rather than at an individual. Having a strong game identity ensures the positioning of a game is very clear to anyone who might be interested in playing. The multilayered approach to the mechanic allows players to exist at different levels of skill and interest and still play the game together.

It is said that "a chain is only as strong as its weakest link" and in this case I suppose we could say that "a group is as involved as their least involved player". When engagement levels of the players differ from one another within the same game, they will be seeking a different experience. By designing broadly for each level of engagement we can ensure that the different types of players get what they desire from the game.

- *Low-intensity players* are most commonly looking for gratification and instant "fun" things that are exciting to do in the moment. This can be achieved through satisfyingly tactile interaction (e.g. those tiles feel very nice to match),] and getting rewarded for small challenges (e.g. solving this simple puzzle made me feel smart). Some players may never get past this stage of engagement with your game and only engage with it because of their friends. This is why for this level it's important to give players plenty of quick engaging actions to do with others.

- *Medium-intensity players* are most commonly looking to explore the boundaries of the game and understand it better. They are in search of depth and new content. This is when players will experiment with different kinds of modes and mechanics and try to find a better way to make other people's experiences better. This can be a transitory phase to being high intensity, but this is also the place where players will stay if life circumstances or skill and desire impede them from being more involved. This is probably where most longer-term engaged players actually stand. They care enough about what the game has to offer, but in a way that is more casual than the very top percentile.

- *High-intensity players* are usually after challenging the structure of the game and showcasing their knowledge about it. If a player has reached "high engagement" they know most about the game and they are looking to either challenge themselves with things like competition or high-difficulty play or they are looking for other ways to show their competence, such as instructing others how to play.

Depending on the kind of game that we aim to create we might cater more to one level of intensity over the other. When the goal is to get as many people enjoying the game as possible even for a short time, low-intensity segments of the audience are most important. Think about hyper-casual games, for example, or even simple party games. When the aim is to get players to engage with the game over a longer period of time, medium intensity is what we are focusing on, trying to show the players that there is depth and value and new content to explore. Think of most mobile games that have a construction meta like *Gardenscapes* or your average *Pokémon* game. If the goal is to create a highly competitive niche game that is not everyone's cup of tea but is deeply enjoyed by those who play it, the high-intensity players are the most important to cater to. These games have steep difficulty curves and lots of complexity that aim to give players not only a sense of achievement when they manage to break through but also gives them plenty of space to feel challenged once they do know everything about the game. An example is the game *Eve Online*.

All this is of course not to say that the more casual games I mentioned have no high-intensity players, but that is not where they focus their efforts. Because of how this funnel works with players going from low to medium to high engagement, games that are meant to be played with other people longer term, like a social game, have to spread their bets a little bit more than single-player games. The aim is to satisfy both low- and high-engagement players to a certain degree where they both see value in returning to play together. This is where the layering is most important. Rather than pushing those players who can't or don't want to be more engaged to have fun, the trick is to offer distinct layers of interaction that can be embraced or ignored depending on what the user wants. Engaging with the deeper systems must be satisfying and useful but not fundamental to the game experience, so those who have the time and desire get more out of the game but not in a way that makes the game unfair. This is a difficult balance to strike of course and it is in many ways the main challenge to face in a multiplayer game. How can the game host and entertain an audience that is not homogeneous? But for more casual social games the "point" of the progression is not always functional gameplay rewards but instead self-expression and abilities that mean players can help each other more.

Integrate social within the game economy

The economy is the backbone of the game, and it concerns itself with everything that can be gained or spent. It extends far beyond the flow of currency; it encapsulates all the resources or items that the game generates and what their value is. For the player, the game economy sits in the background pulling and pushing in ways they might not even realise. But the economy should never be an afterthought for developers.

The easiest way to make sure a game economy is sound is to extract the value of an item from real, quantifiable things. For most games these values are most notably time, money and skill. But multiplayer and especially social multiplayer have access to a fourth dimension of value: social points.

Social points are by nature difficult to quantify as they are derived from the hypothetical "good will" we use to complete social transactions between people. This is of course a parameter a lot more difficult to use than time, money or even skill because unlike those the "value" of social interaction is a lot more subjective but not entirely unquantifiable. And while it is difficult to use, it is important to remember that in a game where players are expected to interact with others, these kinds of transactions are happening whether we want to acknowledge it or not. It is therefore better to factor it all in so we have a better understanding of the true value of actions and items in the game.

In order to understand how social points flow, let's look at a non-game example first. Say that me and my friends are trying to find a good takeout restaurant to order from while having a night in. If I want to suggest my favourite restaurant, I use my existing social points to convince others that it is a good choice. But social transactions are a gamble. If my friends enjoy my pick, I am likely to earn social points and get to pick our food options in the future. But if people don't like my pick, it might be a while before my pick makes top billing again, and I lose some of my social points.

Let's now look at a game example and notice where social transactions happen and why:

- **The buy-in:** Depending on what kind of game one might want to play and the people they are trying to play a game with, the social points spent for people to buy into playing that game will be different. This goes back to previous points of making a game appealing and accessible to a wide audience.
- **The team-up cost:** Once in the game players spend social points in order to match their friend's level in co-op, this applies to lower-intensity players struggling to keep up with their more engaged play partners and to highly engaged players entertaining simpler content for their friend's sake. In this case the player makes an abstraction of their gaming preferences in order to appease their friend.
- **The competition cost:** Competition is by definition a higher intensity activity than cooperation because it involves proving ourselves. Much like the team-up cost, the competition cost is derived from a desire to appease friends, but in this case it is there to keep confrontation within the boundaries of the game.
- **The help cost:** This is the circumstance in which players repeatedly solicit help from their friend either because of the nature of the game (in casual games this can be intrinsically linked to in-app purchases) or because of a difference in game-playing skill (e.g. one player must keep reviving the other when they die).
- **The inconvenience cost:** This is similar to the help cost but is not linked to one person needing the other but rather the fact that multiplayer games can oftentimes feel "inefficient" compared to their solo counterparts, and players pay this "inconvenience cost" in order to gain a social connection with the people they are playing with.

When looking at adding sinks and taps to our diagrams and understanding the flow of the currencies and other items through the game it is important to consider if said actions have an added social cost that would make them more difficult for the player to interact with. This will have a pretty big impact on the value of the reward the player gets out of completing said activity.

Let's consider a more concrete example. Say I want to encourage players to play more PvP (player versus player) matches in a shooter game and as a result of that I am trying to decide what kind of rewards are suitable for someone who is participating in these PvP matches. If we were to make this calculation solely based on time (say for example the reward someone gets from PvE [player versus environment] for 1 minute of play is equal to the reward someone gets for 1 minute of playing PvP) we would severely under-reward the player for their efforts. In the case of a PvP encounter all those extra costs need to be accounted for. The buy-in, the competition cost and the help cost all work out to make PvP a more "valuable" mode to play per minute. This would of course mean that someone playing only PvP will progress faster than someone playing only PvE even if they invest the same amount of time. But as we mentioned before, time is not the only resource being invested in the game ultimately, and players must feel like the reward equals their investment.[1]

The social FTUE

The first-time user experience (or FTUE) of a player is fundamental for all games, being a determining factor in retaining users over time. For premium games the FTUE is there to onboard the player and convince them that the purchase they have made is valuable. Most of the time this means that players will want to keep the game in their library even if they don't play it that much. For F2P (free-to-play) games, however, the FTUE is a lot more fundamental because these games do not get to make any return on investment unless enough players stay in long enough in order to engage with in-app purchases or monetised ads. This is not to say that F2P games only care about getting players to the point of paying, but in their case the retention over multiple days is more important than it is in the case of a premium game. The FTUE is more than just the tutorial, although it ultimately includes it. It's in fact about the entire first experience interacting with a game and it focuses on accomplishing a few clear goals:

- Hook the player
- Teach the player to play
- Give the player a reason to return

Fundamentally, these three things are the cornerstone of what the player must get from their first time playing the game in order to see them return, and while there is definitely a correlation between the first gameplay session and the FTUE they are not intrinsically linked. Sometimes the FTUE might be stretched over a longer period of time and encompass more sessions in order to ease the player into the mechanics and convince them of the game's value. The topic of FTUEs is well studied and there are plenty of sources that explore this in depth and teach how to make a good first-time experience for the user.

Something I feel that is not so often talked about is the social first-time user experience of the player, for those games that do include another player. This is because while there is a lot of thinking behind how people play together once they have already found each other, there is in my opinion a lot of arm-waving involved in how exactly they get to that point. And there is so much more to this first-time social user experience than meets the eye because while the FTUE is something we can control entirely from one person's point of view, the social FTUE is a dialogue between the person initiating the play and the person responding to their call. This means that the structure of it bounces back and forth between the people engaged in it. It then follows that the first-time user experience is actually different for different people if they are to be considered the initiator or the responder to the call. Note that when we are talking about initiator and responder we are not only talking about games that work in pairs, but we assign these roles to the players based on the part they play in the flow. An initiator can have more than one responder or multiple people can play the role of initiator if they try the game out for the first time together in order to try it before they play with their friends.

The initiator must get the following things from their first-time social user experience:

- Clear proof of appeal and social value
- An understanding of how the game is played with other people
- Additional incentives to recommend the game to other people

For the responder, the first-time social user experience is a little simpler. They already have someone who is playing the game who would like them to join, so half of the hard work is already done for us.

- Teach the player how to engage and help their friends
- Provide them with ways to reengage the initiator

If a regular FTUE is a series of steps one player must take, the social FTUE is a dance, and both parts of this dance are vital for the flow to work as intended. Different types of games take different approaches to making sure that the loop from initiator to responder to initiator is closed.

The most important part of the social FTUE is first and foremost picking the right moment to bring people together, and there isn't really a universal answer for this even though certain types of games are more suitable to one approach than another.

Some games decide to limit their play to real multiplayer; think for example party video games like the *Jackbox* packs or even something like *Among Us*. In general games like these have one main difficulty and that is convincing the player to engage their friends without getting to experience it for themselves first. This is why more classic distribution methods and classic marketing work best in their case (like in the case of *Jackbox*), or if luck strikes, the game can become popular out of the blue due to internet virality (like was the case for *Among Us*). While there is nothing wrong with the approach, it's very difficult to get the players to start playing. The social buy-in price is very high, and unless you rely on intensive marketing, brand loyalty or sheer luck, this type of game is hard to get rolling. But this type of setup has its advantages as well, with a huge one being that everyone is on the same footing when they first start playing the game. Sure some may know more about how the game is played from watching other people, but ultimately the social FTUE is the same and it happens concurrently for everyone. There are a lot of advantages in this case:

- The pressure of learning the game is distributed among the players and having the participants explain to each other how to play can be more engaging than a tutorial.
- There is a stronger social obligation to give the game a solid try in order to make the play experience good for everyone.
- Social interaction around an activity can make it a more positive experience, and if the very first experience we have with the game is a successful social experience, we might think more fondly of the game as a whole.

The dynamic created in this kind of game is mostly suitable for easy pick-up-and-play party games, so players can share that experience but not get overwhelmed by the work they have to put in to learn the mechanics. Traditionally these games have no further complexity beyond the simple initial mechanic and there is little progression there aside from potentially unlocking more new modes or getting cosmetics. This is mostly because they want to make sure the players are more or less on the same page when they get to play the game and that means that anything added to the game increases the tension of that first session.

Other games usually keep the social FTUE for later on in the user experience in the interest that the game is theoretically first and foremost a personal experience and only after it becomes a social experience. This applies not only to games that can be played both solo and multiplayer (take for example *Destiny 2*), but it also applies to multiplayer games that have the player match up with or against bots in their very first sessions. This is because, most notably, one cannot have a social experience unless it's with another human, and even though the bot is filling in the functional gap of another player, they are not there to engage the player socially but to engage with them mechanically. This means that the experience while technically multiplayer is still a solo one. A lot of bigger, more complex multiplayer games use this method. It has become more or less standard for players to not encounter other real people until later in their experience, and how transparent the game is about it varies. Some games try to preserve the illusion of playing with or against real people. Take for example a game like *Fortnite* where nobody plays against humans in their first few matches. Other games are more transparent about matching players against bots to complete the training. Some go as far as to make the tutorial a very scripted experience that one has alone before they can proceed to play with others.

The reason why more complex games tend to use this method is two-fold. Firstly, the mechanical complexity makes it overwhelming for a first-timer to be involved with others socially. This means that players would have too much on their minds when learning the game to want to engage with others. Secondly, there's the question of our perceived performance and the game's difficulty. Regardless of how rigorous the matchmaking is, playing with other people means you cannot guarantee the outcome of those few matches. It's no surprise that winning when you first start playing will encourage you to keep going. The positive encouragement of overcoming an obstacle results in people wanting to try their hand at the next thing thrown at them.

An interesting question in the case of fabricating a multiplayer FTUE with bots is whether the player knows they are not playing against real humans, and there are good reasons to consider both faking users or being transparent about bots depending on the situation. On one hand, being upfront about the use of bots can alleviate the pressure on the player to "perform" in their first session, and while wins against bots are not as valuable as wins against players, they can still be rewarding if done right. On the other hand, to "disguise" bots as real users while incredibly difficult boosts the value of those wins while making the experience still manageable for the player, the only caveat being that if people catch on their trust is broken, which invalidates a lot of the benefits of that initial win. Games might decide to go for one over the other for multiple reasons, and it's mostly to do with their audience. Oftentimes these features are tested once the game is already out there in order to improve the first-time user experience.

Another factor to consider in this kind of situation is whether to block other players from joining their friends until the tutorial is over. This has the benefit of keeping the experience controlled, but it has the major disadvantage of making people wait before they can play with their friends.

In my personal experience people do not want to wait to join their friends when they come to a game with the desire to be social. When we tested games in which a single-player tutorial had to be completed before one could join their friends, the results were unsurprisingly negative. We realised that players were just rushing through the content and not actually paying attention or absorbing any information because their goal was to hang out and play and the tutorial was an obstacle. The most efficient way we found is to let people play together from the very beginning as that makes the experience of the responder so much richer and they are as a result much more likely to stick around. Playing the game with someone they already know can lend a lot of advantages in teaching the new player, meaning the game might not even need to put as much effort into doing so. We should instead focus on giving people the tools to have the best social experience and the learning tends to flow from one friend to the other.

Altogether the social FTUE must not be thought of as a separate experience from the rest of the first-time user experience. Instead it has to be waived through the fabric of this experience in order to instil to the player the fact that social is a cornerstone of the game. Ultimately we do not want the player's first interaction with other people to be happenstance. We want to use the design to make that experience as fulfilling as possible and give the players a way to bond socially in the game as soon as possible.

Note

1. One of the tools I use for systems modelling is Machinations.io, as it allows me to very clearly see the connection between the steps taken by the player during a game and what kind of reward is reasonable to offer them based on their performance. The diagram showcases a simplified example of calculating experience points (XP) in a PvP shooter game while incorporating social points into the calculation (see https://my.machinations.io/d/social -economy/53c7584f8c3d11ee8ff60a893d14f349).

chapter 9

The ethics of social game design

Design is a powerful tool. The main purpose of it is to offer solutions to society's problems, and the more we understand the psychology of design. the more we know we can incentivise the target audience to take certain actions. We consider this "good design" because it helps us achieve goals and because even if the experience is net positive for the audience, people still need convincing a lot of the time. Especially when we are talking about using "data-led" approaches to design, it's very easy to slip into a mentality that the result is more important than the means or even that we as designers know better what players need. While not untrue that players can sometimes ruin their own fun by exploiting game systems and being reticent to engage with them, it's far too easy to fall into the trap of "if I could only force them to do X then everything will be great".

While it is true that guiding the player through an experience using psychological principles of design leads to a smoother, more intuitive experience for the player, it's very important that these tools are used in good faith, as I have mentioned throughout this book. The line between persuasion and manipulations is not as obvious as it might seem, especially when there are secondary effects we might not have considered. We should always aim to use design in a positive way, and while making games might not seem like a high-stakes endeavour, as creators of entertainment the emotional impact we can have on people is significant. We have to be very aware of the purposes that games serve in people's lives in order to truly understand the power we hold. People turn to games for comfort and relaxation, they use games to break the ice at parties and build memories with those they love, they play to feel free and experiment with the way they live their lives. But games can also be an escape, a place for people to run away from their day-to-day struggles, a way to drown out the noise of the world. For all of these reasons, what we make can have a huge positive impact on people's lives and social connections. But just as eating too much junk food can turn a treat into an unhealthy lifestyle, the decisions we make when building our games can turn something intended for enjoyment into something that the player cannot stop interacting with even when it is to their overall detriment.

The conversation of ethical design in video games goes beyond the most common discussion about "video game addiction". It's about all the

DOI: 10.1201/9781003314325-12

things that the player might feel compelled to do without consideration. Certain demographic groups are also more susceptible to these psychological design tactics, be it because of their history with addictive behaviours, spending habits, age and other factors. All of these can affect a person's ability to discern when these "tactics" are being used on them.

Most commonly we see the conversation of ethical design in video games talked about in the context of the well-being of children and adolescent and that is an important discussion to have. The conversation about how much free time one is compelled to spend on a video game is complex. The discussion must always be about how the time spent in the game affects the player's quality of life. The time itself might not be the actual factor to determine if playing ends up being an overall gain or loss. We know that all dopamine-inducing activities can be overused to the point when they become a crutch rather than an enjoyable pastime, so while there is definitely more nuance on the subject than we often see in media, it would be unfair not to address it. While I will not explore this much further in this book, as it goes beyond the scope of it there is plenty of literature on the subject that sheds a lot of light on the matter.[1]

Another side of manipulative design discussion explores the way people spend money in games, from gambling games to video game loot boxes and even microtransactions that use predatory marketing strategies to encourage people to keep spending more even when they might not be able to afford it. As discussed earlier, certain groups of people are naturally more predisposed to fall into the traps of unethically designed systems. There is a general misconception from players (and even some industry people) that equates the concepts of microtransactions and free-to-play mechanics with these kinds of predatory practices. In reality we all know that games have to make money one way or another and it all boils down to value. If players have gained value from the product enough to justify spending the money, then it is a transaction like any other. If on the other hand, players feel like they cannot get enough value from the game but mechanics try to pressure them into spending their money, that becomes more ethically grey and therefore we should tread carefully. There is a wealth of literature that goes deeper into the ethics of monetisation practices especially in free-to-play.

One of the things that is less frequently talked about I believe is the ethics of social game design and the impact a game can have on the real-world relationships of the people playing. In previous chapters we discussed social points and how people use them as currency in order to engage with others during the game. In this chapter I will like to discuss the ability of a game to influence relationships and how important it is that we are aware of the social space we are harbouring.

How do ethics play into social design?

Let's start by analysing a game that already exists to explore what I believe to have examples of unethical social design. In the mobile game *Coin Master* there are two main components of the core loop: spinning the fruit machine and building your village. Every time the player spins there are several outcomes possible:

- They can win larger stacks of coins.
- They can win more "spins".
- They can win a shield (up to three available at the time).
- They can get the ability to attack someone's village.
- They can gain the ability to steal from the "Coin Master" (the person with the most coins that you know).
- They can get a compensatory "small win" if no symbols match.[2]

With the money they earn the player can build and upgrade their village. After upgrading the village for a certain amount of time, the player has a prestige moment where they move on to a new village they can work on building up. Moving from one village to another in the prestige moment is purely a visual milestone, but it serves as a way to "checkpoint" the player's progress. In classic game economy fashion, the more the player progresses through the game the more expensive the building and upgrading the town becomes. This is the core of the game progression: players aim to get to the next prestige point both to get access to new village visual content and to "bank" all the currency they have invested so far.

The secondary layer of the game is attacking other players or stealing from them (they are technically different mechanics but socially they serve a very similar purpose). Like other mobile games, *Coin Master* will ask the player to connect their Facebook account in order to play socially, and players are heavily incentivised to do so even before the player really knows anything about the game. While connecting to social media at the beginning of the very first session is not unique to this game, due to the nature of the interactions possible, the incentive to connect to Facebook takes a slightly different meaning for the player. People are encouraged to set back other people's progress in order to proceed themselves, and because these are people that the player might know personally, it has an opportunity to affect their relationship.

Apart from the fact that the social game mechanic is entirely antagonistic in nature, there is also no way for the player to choose to avoid it (if the fruit machine spins an attack or a steal you have to do it to continue playing). This paired with the addictive nature of the gambling-like mechanic, the players can be incentivised to become more and more attached to the dopamine hit the game gives them and see their actions less and less as affecting others. Furthermore, as the player progresses through the game as well, the milestones for investing your currency get further and further apart, increasing the stakes. This means that people need to play more frequently be more aggressive, and potentially invest their own real-world money. The game encourages players to target their friends and singles out the "richest" player as the most efficient target for those who want to progress quickly. In other words, the game creates an environment of extreme peer pressure. Let's see how it does so.

Using social reengagement unethically

In previous chapters we discussed how we can use social reengagement to encourage players to return to the game. The idea behind this is that if we all have a great time playing a game together chances are we are gonna keep reminding each other of the game's existence. This will lead to habits of play and using the game as a joint pastime, as part of our "hanging out" routine. There is however a darker side to social reengagement, and it can be observed in *Coin Master*.

When the player is away from their game for an extended period of time, they risk other players setting back their progress by attacking or stealing from them. This creates a high-tension social environment where players return to the game not so much because they are having great fun interacting with others but because they are afraid of what others can do to them while they are away from the game. This method of engagement can also become a gateway for people to pick on or bully a single person. If a group of ill-intended people were to "team up" against a specific person, they could keep destroying everything this person builds in a matter of minutes.

It might seem like an overreaction to assume that these kinds of mechanics are anything else than a little bit of banter among friends, especially as this is "just a game" and the stakes are not as high as they might be otherwise, but let's analyse this for a moment. As designers we hold the keys to a lot of psychological "tricks" that we want to use in order to get the players to behave in a way that makes them engage with the game. Designing in good faith implies that we have the player's best interest at heart (i.e. we want the experience of playing to be a net positive on their lives). When those psychological design techniques involve other people, designing in good faith is about what role we play in the social lives of people, and this goes far beyond the edges of the screen. We must always ask ourselves:

- What kind of behaviours are we enabling?
- What kind of community are we building?
- What is the psychological impact of someone playing this game with others?

Let's look at those questions through the lens of *Coin Master.*

What behaviours is it enabling? The social behaviour most success-ful in *Coin Master* is a mercenary attitude toward the game and the way you progress. Being antagonistic is inevitable, so what happens is those who hate the feeling don't continue playing and those who like it have the opportunity and incentive to become more and more aggressive over time.

What kind of community is it building? Because of the kind of people the game is attracting and enabling, the community reflects this merce-nary attitude. Furthermore, because the game is in direct connection with the player's Facebook friend list, the game community affects the real-world social sphere of the players. Players might even be incentivised to "unfriend" someone because of their in-game behaviour.

What is the psychological impact of someone playing this game with others? While it's difficult to say for sure what value players are getting out of playing the game without insider knowledge and user research, it's clear to see that the addictive nature of the gambling mechanics com-bined with an antagonistic social interaction mechanic has the potential to be detrimental for the user's mental health. How much the contents of the game affect the player is completely derived from how involved they are in the game, but let us not forget that like in the case of any type of gambling certain people are more vulnerable and more susceptible to it. But would the impact still be negative if we subtracted the fruit machine mechanic and replaced it with something more akin to a mobile casual mechanic like a match three? I believe the results would still be simi-lar. The "gambling" core of the game goes beyond the fact that the main mechanic is entirely luck-based, and it is more about the flow of currency in the game, more poignantly the ability to lose the money you invested or earned so far.

We can recognise therefore how social engagement in this case is used in damaging ways that we could call unethical but are all examples this obvious? No! As designers we love solving problems, but there are so many ways to look at the same problem that will lead you to a different result. The line between persuasion and manipulation relies on the empa-thy the designer has for their audience and looking to solve the problem from their point of view. Later in this chapter we will discuss how best to use empathy in order to make sure we are using our design abilities in good faith.

Peer pressure and spending habits

Games are no strangers to using other people as an example to make you aspire to something and use that in order to leverage purchases; the whole of society does this in fact. We are more likely to desire that new kitchen gadget if our friend who bakes delicious cakes recommends it to us. In many cases we look to those around us to give us a true value assessment of what they have spent their money on and if it would be worth it for us to invest the money.

In previous chapters we discussed how people we know influence the kind of games we are willing to play, but how does this same relationship with people affect the way that we engage financially with the game after we have already started playing? Outside influence on our in-game spending habits tends to fall in one of the following categories:

- Fear of missing out
- Compensating for a lack of time or skill
- Vanity and fitting in

Fear of missing out (FOMO) is the desire to have access to the same things that others have, for example, downloadable content (DLC) or a specific gun. In this situation one player might feel compelled to spend extra money in order to get the extras on the game that they wouldn't have bought if their friends or their favourite streamer didn't recommend it. This kind of external incentive is focused on the experience of playing the game and how much better the game would be if only you had access to this extra content. Would I have more fun if I got that gun? Would I understand the main story better if I got the DLC? Developers can create an elevated state of "missing out" either by pushing adverts through streamers and YouTubers, limiting product availability (most commonly based on time) or promoting "aspirational figures" where people who are already enjoying that exclusive content are shown to be having so much more fun. While these methods are salesy and they can be a bit pushy at times, I would not consider them unethical. The reason being that there is value in the content that the developer is trying to prove to the player through the medium, for example. be it from a friend, a streamer or a cool fellow player spotted inside the game.

Being able to compensate for skill or a lack of time to play is often frowned upon by players. Having the ability to skip gameplay and just pay in order to get further faster is considered poor sportsmanship, especially in a PvP setting. The external incentive here is to be able to progress without investing time and stressing over difficult challenges. This desire to use money to skip content is more or less the flip side of the FOMO investment. In this case the player cares more about the end result and less about the journey. They might choose to do this for many reasons: maybe they are busier than their friends but still want to play together, maybe this is their secondary account and they care more about the end game, maybe they get satisfaction from reaching goals quicker and don't care about the methods used to reach them. Allowing players to use currency to shortcut skilful gameplay is not inherently "evil" in many ways; it could be considered an accommodation for those who need the help to be able to use it. It can however become dangerous when the main method to succeed at the game is exclusively through this added paid content, because at that point it is no longer optional. If the season's paid gun is ten times more powerful than any other gun and there is no way to get it other than through paying, that creates a "pay to win" social environment that can be toxic and affect the player financially as a result.

Spending money on vanity items is exclusively socially motivated. Players spend their money on skins and other cosmetics in order to show their social status and adherence to the group. This is where peer pressure can really create an environment where players want to either outdo each other or they will spend any amount of money to not be the odd one out. This is an area where developers can leverage their social status and social relationships in order to increase their profits. Just as nobody wants to be the only kid in high school wearing the "wrong" kind of sneakers, nobody wants to be the only *League of Legends* player in the lineup without a skin. Pushing people to purchase vanity items can become unethical when the developers are exacerbating the negative interactions already existing in a group to maximise profits.

This is what happens in the *Coin Master* example. Of course the village upgrade stands in for the main progression mechanism in the game, but ultimately it is a vanity item, it is there to say "look how far I've made it". *Coin Master* pushes players who already have a tendency to push other people's buttons for self-enjoyment to do so in an environment where they are rewarded for it. The financial benefit for the game is twofold: the person attacking might feel incentivised to push further to the next prestige point and the people who they have just attacked have little opportunity to retaliate. The person who is getting attacked might be incentivised to spend money in order to protect their past investment or be able to recuperate the amount lost without spending even more time on the game.

The "need" for entertainment

The word "unethical" is thrown around a lot, same with the word "manipulation". There is an expected push and pull of society that needs to rely on the idea of efficiently selling products and services to consumers. Games are a form of art and entertainment and therefore their monetary value has always been questioned by the public. Is the £60 you pay for a game on launch day a fair price or are you seduced by marketing into buying something you "don't need"? Are the microtransactions in a free-to-play game "reasonable" to offer to the player given that the whole design behind them is that players are more likely to spend small amounts of money frequently than bigger lump sums? Is it unethical to offer players the option to buy an item that would otherwise take players hours to farm had they not invested their real money into it? The conversation on this topic is as you might expect, more nuanced than it might look.

Let's discuss the nature of games as entertainment artefacts. In theory, play is not "necessary" for humans to survive. In Maslow's hierarchy of needs, play straddles the line between a psychological need and self-actualisation. This is why leisure trends always go down the list of things to do and invest money in, but this is not to say that games and play in general are not important. I would argue that "needs" are not as hierarchical as we might think. Even when we might not have some of our basic needs met, people indulge in ways of entertaining themselves in order to sweeten the situation. I always like to believe that we all have the right to entertainment and this is why making it accessible for people in all kinds of situations is fantastic. Free-to-play games are a good example of making something previously very inaccessible available to everyone. Games will unfortunately never solve world hunger, but they might just manage to make people a little bit happier when times are hard. It is therefore important for us to understand this place we have in people's lives both in order to understand the value of the things we make and to understand that the people we are designing for are varied and their desire for play can sometimes come from this need to escape. We want to make sure that people's mentality around play is healthy and that while we want to design for engagement and try to make profitable games, there is a clear way for the players to stop and plenty of moments to digest their decisions of investing. Let's explore a fictional example.

Farming Simulation X is a top-down farm management game. In the game the player takes actions to take care of crops, sell the products they make for a profit and expand their farm in order to grow new crops. In this game the ability of a player to perform actions is done based on an energy mechanic. This means that players can only do so much before they need to stop and recharge over a period of time. Timed mechanics can be a force for good especially to limit the amount of continuous active play. They also serve as a reason to return to the game, as we previously discussed throughout this book. It is also fairly common practice that these kinds of games will offer the ability to speed up processes or buy more energy by using real money. This is not unethical in nature, although it can be seen as a pay-to-win mechanic. This method becomes dangerous however the moment the player feels like they are being cornered to use their money in order to proceed at all or that they are gonna lose their progress if they don't invest their money (this is the case of loss aversion we saw in the *Coin Master* example).

Especially when we are talking about free-to-play, the mentality should not be let's get everyone playing to eventually pay, as if it was a premium game where players just "pay later". Instead the idea is to offer the users a multitude of avenues to engage with the product should they wish to because unlike premium games the pool of people playing is often larger, and therefore even if only a portion of that audience pays it can still be enough to sustain those who made it.

So what are some of these blockers that try to force the players to spend:

- Reliance on purchasable items to proceed
- Waiting times that become unreasonable
- User interface (UI) pop-ups for purchases that can't be easily dismissed
- Fake involvement of friends to encourage spending

All of these techniques evolve from common game design techniques but end up being taken a step too far. It follows basic game balancing theory that things should get harder to achieve for the player so that the progression curve follows from easy to more difficult as the player goes on, but this kind of design must cap at some point. There is a certain point beyond which it becomes unreasonable to expect the player to wait for their "town to get upgraded" or their "energy to return". Past this reasonable amount of time the purchase becomes "necessary" even if there is another way around. What we are saying through this mechanic is that "unless you are a paying customer or you have time to spare, we don't want you here". Same goes for the UI that feels impossible to exit. It's one thing to de-emphasise the close button a little bit in order to convince ourselves that the player definitely noticed and understood the opportunity to purchase something (although some UI designers may debate this is an antiquated and bad technique). It is a completely different thing however to use unintuitive UI for the close button or use a fake close button that instead of closing the pop-up takes you to a purchase page (a practice used a lot more in recent times especially in the case of in-game adverts for other apps of games, where fake timers and close buttons take you to the storefront). The truth is that none of these techniques will work on those who are not already predisposed to falling into these kinds of "traps". If a pop-up comes up that asks me to spend money and I cannot seem to easily close it, I will just close the entire app and maybe never return. Meanwhile if I am in a vulnerable position and the same pop-up stands between me and the little bit of joy I get from interacting with this game I am more likely to spend my money. These practices are not unethical just because the players "can't" get around them easily, they are unethical because it takes will to get around them and those who are harmed by the insidious design are those who are already vulnerable.

Feedback with compassion

In today's society it might feel like there will always be a struggle between makers and consumers. Society has taught us that in order to be successful we have to push our audiences to engage and consume more and more. We measure our success not only in financial profits but also in the frequency and time spent inside the game. Metrics in general are pivotal to many companies. Although metrics give us insight about "how well we are doing", they do not tell us "how to do well". Designing solely through the lens of numbers reduces people to points of data that tell no story about what purpose the game serves in their lives and what is the way that their experiences could be improved. Design goals should therefore always be about the player first and secondarily look at the potential impact to the metrics. Rather than saying "We want to increase retention by 5%" we should say "We want to make sure the player understands the replay value of the game in their first session so they are more likely to return". The meaning of this is theoretically the same, but when we think more about "what we could do for the player" and less about "how to get the player to do what we want" we can start seeing the design process as more of a dialogue than a monologue.

This way of designing boils down to two main things:

1. Communicating with the audience
2. Having empathy for your players

Communication with your audience ensures that we understand our product in a completely different light because we will always be seeing our product from the inside looking out. Empathy makes us respond to the user's concerns with warmth by trying to put ourselves in their shoes. The two are essential and they must always be considered together. Communication without empathy leads to dismissed feedback and empathy without communication leaves us with more questions than answers and can create an inability to make decisions.

In the book *Thanks for the Feedback*, the authors Stone and Heen talk about how people receive feedback in the context of interpersonal relationships. They suggest that it is us who ultimately have the least amount of information about ourselves and our own behaviours, and therefore we need others as points of reference to understand the whole picture. Let's look at this using an analogy: we as people never really get to perceive ourselves and our facial expressions, so when someone tells us some news and suggests we had a bad reaction to what they said we cannot accurately assess what that reaction was. We might think to ourselves "I didn't say or do anything", but the expression on our faces said it all.

Expanding upon the idea that we are the least aware of ourselves because of our unique point of view, I think the same is true of the products we create. From the inside, many things we do seem like good ideas. We look at our solutions as little pieces of the puzzle and we try to fit it all into this elegant grand design. From this position, hearing players say something like "I feel like I have been grinding long enough. I deserve to continue without having to pay" could stir an emotional reaction in us: "Haven't they already played this game for free so far? Isn't my work worth as much as a cup of coffee?" The expression in the game of our desire to be recognised for our work is a big ugly pop-up that tries to force the player to pay before they can proceed. "Fine, if you don't respect my work I will not respect your time and wish not to spend money". The player is appalled, seeing our expressions from the outside looking in. They are thinking "Is that how you treat me after investing my precious time playing this game for so long?" We are left dumbfounded, the player is disappointed and in the end we didn't make any more money either. This is what happens when we are both not communicating enough and reacting with low empathy towards the little feedback we receive.

In order to avoid this we need to cultivate a mentality where we ask questions of the player in order to understand their point of view fully, and we approach those answers with understanding and compassion. A thought experiment I like to do sometimes is treating your user as a friend. Say you get a negative review on your storefront: "This game sucks! I spent 100 hours and I just feel like I wasted my time. The ending was garbage". What we might be inclined to hear as the developer is "You suck! Your work sucks! I regret spending my time and my hard-earned money on this!" But if I was this person's friend, what I would understand would be quite different: "Man, I really wanted to love this game. I spent my time and my money on it, and I was sure I was going to love it. By the end of it the game did not fulfil me, and it felt like the game disrespected my investment by delivering a poorly thought-out rushed ending".

While compassion is all about being able to understand someone else's feelings, it paradoxically helps us get over our own strong emotional reaction to feedback. If we know they are not trying to hurt our feelings and instead they are trying to express their own, we will be more likely to listen to what they are saying rather than reacting to how they are saying it. I am not suggesting that we should take emotion out of feedback, but rather we should understand that the emotion the feedback is delivered with is just more information we can use. Let's go back to the bad storefront review. The player says the "ending is garbage". They use strong language to indicate emotions: "I am disappointed". If we use the feelings as a context for what the player is saying we can uncover more about the feedback. This player managed to reach the ending. This means they got a lot further than most people, so to some degree they must have found the game compelling. Secondly, their feeling of disappointment was so strong that they felt the need to express themselves in a review. This means that their expectations were high and the content didn't hit the mark. Ideally we could reach out to the player and ask them more questions, but even through the little we have we can tell more about this person's feedback and create a profile for them which allows us to empathise with their situation and design better for them and others like them.

Compassionate design is the road to ethical design, but it is not the only requirement. Sometimes we are blinded to the impact of our own solutions. With all the goodwill in the world we can make decisions that affect the player negatively and create tension. This is why purposeful ethical design is important. It is not enough to have the desire to make ethical decisions. It's about making sure we don't make unethical decisions by accident. All design changes have a domino effect; one harmless change here can cascade into an issue somewhere else. This is why we need to remain vigilant and keep ourselves aware of the bigger picture of our entire product.

So can a design be considered unethical if the harmful effect was unintended? I would say the answer is yes. Just because something is done by accident it does not mean it did not have real repercussions on the people using it. Furthermore, just because we are unaware of the negative effect something has on people, it does not mean that it is not an unethical decision to make in the first place. It is our duty as makers to be vigilant and educated on these matters and do our best whenever we can and rectify our mistakes as soon as possible while learning from them. The easiest way of making sure a practice is ethical is to translate it to a "real-life" scenario. When we do so the cracks start to show a lot clearer.

Translate it to real life

Let's explore how a real-life situation can serve us in exploring the ethics of our methods. Say that I am making a game show, and I am inviting you and your friends to take part. The goal of this game show is simple: players must share the resources provided by the production crew to improve their homes and whoever makes the most out of the resources receives recognition and a prize for that week. But there is a catch of course. In order to make the content more interesting contestants are encouraged to steal from each other when nobody's looking. The game show rewards it as the "correct way to play". This being the situation, would you still take the offer, and furthermore would you still bring all your friends to join you? What if I didn't tell you all the rules of the game show before you started and convinced you to sign up your friends for the opportunity of playing? Of course this kind of real-life scenario is an exaggerated one, but it does highlight through its ridiculousness the key inflection points that cause a situation like this to be unethical to those participating:

- Abusing pre-existing social connections between people
- Not being upfront about the rules and contents
- Creating an environment where in order to succeed you have to take advantage of others

The reason to translate a scenario to real life is to make us aware of the social situation we put our players in, even if it is exaggerated. All social situations shine differently when we think of them in "practical" face-to-face scenarios and interactions, because there is no abstraction between one person and the other, there is no barrier of technology. When translating a social situation to real life it can be difficult sometimes to find a one-to-one plausible equivalent, but it does not matter how contrived and ridiculous the "real-life" example is. The one thing we need to always keep in mind is that the social stakes are as similar as possible. Say for example you are looking to better understand how your first-person shooter game encourages people to collaborate with their team during a match. The equivalent of this situation is not a real-life combat scenario, the social stakes would be too high; your game is not a matter of life and death. Instead the most likely team behaves like a team of people playing laser tag. A real-life scenario will have higher social tension by default because of the aforementioned lack of anonymity. It then follows that the situation itself should be of equal consequence to the players.

As the designers of things that people are meant to interact with in a social way, we hold incredible power, and the games we make end up playing two different roles in this social equation.

1. That of the "environment", the possibility space, what the player is able to do and what the overall goal is.
2. That of the facilitator, a virtual "third" person in this conversation with technology that the social pair communicates with jointly and independently, and that emotionally instigates the people to either cooperate or be in competition.

Keeping that in mind when imagining the social situations in the game as real-life interactions, we might think of the "systems" as being both the place that accommodates the actions and as another "character" who through their actions and constant observation change the way people behave with each other. In the previous example, the game will not only be the set of the game show with resources and rules, but it will also be the overly enthusiastic presenter who shoves a microphone in the face of the contestants whenever they can to get their emotions on camera.

The game as an ethical social environment

When we talk about building an ethical social environment for our players we are not talking about a place that does not allow disagreement or encourage competition, instead we are talking about an environment that does not reward toxic behaviours and in fact actively discourages them. Both disagreement and competition are healthy parts of the human social experience. When we eliminate tensions like this we run the risk of censoring the kind of relationships and interactions players would like to have with each other and that in its own way is potentially problematic.

The dos and don'ts of what creates an ethically designed social environment are hard to pin down as they are very specific. The audience and the type of game will dictate how much or how little the game enforces rules on their social interaction. But I would say that while there are no clear answers, there are definitely some best practices to follow:

- **Encouraging positive social interaction**: This can take the form of commendations for the people you play with, mechanics that reward cooperation and ways to make the competition more friendly.
- **Discouraging negative social interaction**: This can take the form of not allowing specific words in your chat, not employing mechanics where one player benefits at the expense of the others and in more extreme situations punishing improper behaviours with bans.
- **Giving the player control to protect themselves**: This can take the form of players being able to report other players if they have been harassed, but it can also be ways to allow them to control how much interaction they are happy to have with other players, things like being able to turn off the chat in a game.
- **Be upfront with your rules**: This can take the form of spelling out to the players what kind of behaviours are acceptable, but it's also about giving the community the power to enforce your rules in order to establish a safe environment.

These guidelines are not perfect and they are not new, but they help establish an environment that is more likely to harbour positive social interaction and that is really all we can hope for. Beyond a certain point, designing the environment will have to become reactive to the issue that this particular group of people is facing. The truth is that social relationships are too complex to predict, and the goal is not to tell people how to engage with each other but rather to harbour their relationships as they are in a way that is non-destructive to others involved. This is of course particularly hard to do, and this is why there are no hard and fast rules.

Fostering a positive environment for people goes beyond the design of the game. It becomes more about community management and how doing that work tactfully and with compassion and devotion to your audience is very important. Although discussing the details of community management goes beyond the scope of this book, there are certain things that developers should always remember about the audience they are making things for.

- **There will always be antagonists, use their powers for good**. Some members of your audience will gain extreme pleasure and entertainment from breaking down your social rules and the game in general. These people can be perceived as a nuisance. While some of them are actually detrimental to the overall environment and might need close management, some just live for attention, and as developers we can use this in a way beneficial to our cause. Fostering relationships even with the most problematic of audience members can tell you a lot about what kind of environment you have built. It can teach you about the weaknesses in your systems and the emergent social behaviours in your game.
- **Build the social environment to welcome those who fit your goals**. Something about community work is that people are never in complete agreement. It's impossible to accommodate everyone's desires for different kinds of social interactions. Some might want your game to be more competitive, while others will want to have no competition because it stresses them out. There will never be a way to satisfy everyone 100%. Of course aiming to keep the core of your audience happy is important, and part of it is offering people a choice in what they can engage with. But ultimately it is the development team that gets to decide what type of social environment they want to build, and that will not appeal to everyone.
- **Be responsive, not reactive**. It goes without saying that once the game is out of your hands you will discover things about the social environment in your game that you could not have anticipated. As developers we can do our best to design an experience, but we can only understand it truly when we see people using it. In this case when certain issues pop up the temptation is to deal with them as quickly as possible, but this runs the risk of rushing into a suboptimal solution without considering the bigger picture. Some small changes can alter an already existing social environment pretty drastically and cause more damage than good that will ultimately be hard or impossible to undo.

At the end of the day it's important to remember that while we influence our audience with the things we, do we do not exert control and we should never really aim to. The only control we should display is about the hard boundaries of what is acceptable in the community. Beyond that, it is our duty to foster and encourage social behaviour by offering an environment where people can build and enhance the relationships they want to have without fear of how that environment might affect them negatively.

The game as an ethical interlocutor in player relationships

Beyond just being the space where players manifest their relationships as previously mentioned, the game also plays the role of a hypothetical third person in a two-person conversation. This can take multiple forms depending on the game, and it can even be all of them depending on the situation.

- **The translator**: The game interprets the intentions of one player from their interaction with the systems and then aims to "translate" said intentions as accurately as possible to the other person. This manifests more practically in what kind of tools of communication the game offers the player (ignoring other routes of communication outside of the game). This includes chat boxes, emotes and any other ways of communication inside the game.
- **The initiator**: The game can play the role of the social initiator in these "conversations". For example, the game can encourage people to communicate with others either through requiring cooperation or mechanics that reward and encourage communication, giving players plenty of ways and reasons to meet new people.
- **The referee**: The game is there to enforce the rules of competition between the players and it is also there to make sure that everyone is being afforded the right kind of rewards for being a valuable part of the team. This includes the rules of deciding how many points one gets for assisting a teammate during a match, but it's also about the kind of punishment one gets for breaking the code of conduct.

In all of these cases the game is using its design to be a third party in the conversation, and in all of these cases there is opportunity for the game to be both good and bad. In the case of the translator, for example, the game can misrepresent others willingly or unwillingly, in the case of the initiator the game can be pushing the players into communications they are not comfortable with and in the case of the referee the game can be unfair or uncaring about how the rules are being applied affect the individual.

What's most important overall is making sure that we are aware of all the ways in which design can affect user interaction and that we are mindful of all the things that one can do that are detrimental. Oftentimes being aware of these pitfalls makes us able to avoid them and by extent makes our design more ethical.

How to approach user experience design ethically: Interview with Patricia Margarit Castelló

I met Patricia Margarit Castelló on a panel about gamification, and from our first conversations I could immediately tell we had a lot in common. One of the things that most excited me to conduct this interview was her experience with games for change and her love for ethics in video games. She and I are really passionate about treating users and the world with care, and her experience lends a lot to this chapter.

Patricia Margarit Castelló: My name is Patricia. I'm from Spain but I've been living and working in the Netherlands for eight years. Back in Spain I studied a Bachelor of Fine Arts with a focus on game design at Universitat Politècnica de València, and it's when I got interested in serious games for the first time. I have always loved games and behavioural psychology, so to discover a combination of both of these things existed was mind-blowing. I fell in love immediately and then from that point I focused on this topic both in my studies and my work.

   After my BA I enrolled in a master's program in multimedia and visual arts so I could learn more about interactivity, user experience and the ethical side of gaming. During that time I started actually creating games for change. The first one, called *Rita Attacks*, was made in a group and it was showcased at a protest against the destruction of a historical neighbourhood in Valencia which is called El Cabanyal, and that game got a lot of attention because it was this huge political and social issue. It was a collaborative video game video mapped on a building. Hundreds of people gathered together to play the game with their voices because we used a sound interface. After this I got a scholarship in Austria for one year to specialise on the topic in the master's program interfaces cultures at Kunstuniversität Linz. My master's thesis was about how to change and boost behaviours through video games, and as a result I created a video game called *Eisenbahnbrücke's Nightmare*. After that, I got invited to showcase it in the Ars Electronica Festival, which is the largest electronic arts festival in Europe. The project was heavily influenced by the one I did in Valencia, but on a big screen instead of on a building and with a different process. The topic I explored was the destruction of a historical bridge due to political and social reasons, and as last time this was a big topic in the city I was living in with some people in favour and others against it.

After my studies I moved to Amsterdam and worked as a UX [user experience] designer and content creator of a small company called Hyko. The product was a polar-bear-shaped lamp connected to an app, containing a lot of games and interactive stories to teach children up to ten years old about global warming and what they could do to help fight against it. After this I started my job as UX designer for Fairphone, my current position, which is an electronics company that aims to make the entire industry act more responsibly and ethically both towards the consumer and the people making these components. And of course I keep creating games for change on the side.

Ioana-Iulia Cazacu: Your interest in ethics and psychology of games is something that drew me to interview you because I find it fascinating as well, and more generally applicable than just in serious games. I think games work with people's brains and it's all psychology, even if we use these "tricks" intentionally or not. But I find the name "serious games" interesting and I have noticed that there's almost a tension between something being meaningful in this way and it being "fun" or engaging. I would love to know your perspective, if there is tension between game designers and people who bring other kinds of expertise to the table.

Patricia Margarit Castelló: Yes indeed it is super interesting because the name "serious" is in theory the opposite of "fun". It's like you cannot be both, (you can) but is what most people think. People tend to have a very simplistic and outdated view on serious games (like those programs trying to teach you maths in school), but modern serious games do so much more. I firmly believe that serious games can be fun and engaging like you said; it's why I do this. The games I created try to reach people emotionally in order to boost behaviours and to raise awareness. Interactivity can help you reach people more; it allows you to speak to their emotions. When people are engaged and actively participating in something they find interesting they are more likely to listen to the message you put forward, at least that's my opinion.

But you are right about the tension of the two halves of these kinds of games. My experience of working with other people was super interesting because we all had different opinions about it and different backgrounds. Some of my colleagues believed that serious games needed to be super philosophical, while others thought the opposite, that heavy topics were not to be considered because they cannot be made fun. I think you can take the best of both worlds, but of course it's not easy. That's the challenge!

It's also something that does not get written about as much as mainstream games do. There is not as much literature to do with serious games design except for the more academic-type articles.

Ioana-Iulia Cazacu: And that is why I think it's important we pull some of these academic ideas into the commonly used vernacular of design, I guess. As video games mature as a medium we find more ways to use them, but so far I think this area has been less explored than others.

Patricia Margarit Castelló: Indeed, there is a lot of game theory that is applicable in this case too like it is in other games, but there is less practical writing about it. I think fewer people do this. For example, I was the first one at my university in Valencia to write a master's thesis on the topic, and it's a huge university. That's one of the reasons I think it's so important to discuss this topic and explore it, to give it more visibility. It's what I am aiming to do.

Ioana-Iulia Cazacu: So you told us about what attracted you to the topic of games for change, but I was wondering if we could pull it a little bit back and talk about what attracted you to games in general and especially your memories of playing games with other people.

Patricia Margarit Castelló: I am of course a gamer at heart. I love doing many things, but gaming remains my biggest passion. I enjoy many different genres, from horror to farming, but my favourite aspect about games is when you can play them with other people, and I used to play MMORPGs [massively multiplayer online role-playing games] a lot.

For many years, I played *Ragnarok Online* and it's how I met my boyfriend. We have been together for 17 years and counting. I used to play a lot of competitive *World of Warcraft* and I was in one of the top guilds in Spain. I also used to play *Guild Wars 2*, but with some of these games I stuck with more than I did with others.

Of course I also like non-MMORPGs that have a co-op option. I love *Don't Starve Together*, *Terraria*, *Monster Hunter* … games where you can play alone but you also have the option to play together with other people. My boyfriend and I usually play together and I also have a group of friends that I play games with. Sometimes we just chat and play single-player games, but I find that we enjoy gaming the most when we play together. Games are an essential and basic part of human relationship establishment like mentioned in the book *Homo Ludens*,[3] so the social aspect of games is very important to me. I also like TTRPGs [tabletop role-playing games], which are similar in principle but not in a video game format. So yeah, I would say that's my background.

Ioana-Iulia Cazacu: It's interesting to see how people have used games throughout their lives to communicate and bond with other people. I like asking that question. I feel like it talks about a certain kind of relationship that people wouldn't be able to build outside of playing games with someone. Do you find that the games help you in some sort of way to establish a different kind of relationship with people or do you think it's just enhancing the relationship you already have with the people you know?

Patricia Margarit Castelló: I think it's a bit of both. With people I already knew from school, for example, we use games to enhance our relationship and spend time together. I'm currently living in the Netherlands and many of my friends are still in Spain so I cannot meet with them every weekend as we used to. Instead we get together to play games and chat in Discord. We're still hanging out, just not in the real world. But other friends of mine I made in games and we never met in real life or maybe just once or twice. In this case we got to know each other in the context of games, and of course this kind of relationship is different.

The way I see it, games are giving me an opportunity to get to know new people in this different way but also spend quality time with the ones I already know. I consider myself quite social and I really enjoy this aspect of games, making new friends and getting to know each other. Games give me a really good opportunity to understand others and their points of view. It helps me to expand my horizons, especially by meeting people I could never meet by proximity, people with different cultural backgrounds and life stories.

Ioana-Iulia Cazacu: So given we have talked about mainstream games and your history with purposeful games I was curious if you could tell us something you have learned about in making games for change that you think are generally applicable lessons that anyone can use in their day-to-day development work?

Patricia Margarit Castelló: Something super important for me is to remain humble, because you may actually know less than you think. Do not fall prey to the ego and think "I know it all! I'm going to design a game about this topic and it's going to be perfect because of reasons". Take the appropriate time to do the research and really distance yourself from the topic and really have a look at the full scope of what you are trying to portray. For me that initial phase of in-depth research is super important whenever making something that uses psychological techniques to boost or change behaviours. It's the ethical thing to do, you have that responsibility to the audience. But I also think it makes for a more powerful message integrated into the fabric of the game which applies to any kind of game. Staying humble enables you to really think about the target audience in the goal. Otherwise you may fall in all kinds of pitfalls and let ego drive decisions. I think it happens more often than people admit to. It's not so easy to distance yourself from your opinions and try to stay objective and to get a full list of everything. But I believe the results to be worth it.

Another important point is to always try to be mindful of ethics. Something as simple as a line of text or a button placement can make a difference. As makers of games we are focused on encouraging and discouraging certain behaviours. With games for change of course there is even more of a message behind it, but the applications are the same. So, for example, when I was working on the smart lamp at Hyko, we wanted to explain better to kids that they need to turn off the lights whenever they go out of the room to save energy. So let's say you tell them: "If you turn the lights off, you will save the environment". Well, that is not really true; it's quite a bold statement to make. So even though we were trying to get them to do something "good" we have the responsibility when designing things in a way that we do not manipulate.

I believe that to be an incredibly important factor to take into account: To always try to design in a way that is mindful and very respectful of your audience's wants and desires outside of your game. "Ethical" is a name for it, but you could also call it "honest". And it's important to pay attention to this because otherwise you risk falling into manipulation. There is a very thin line between encouraging behaviours and actual manipulation; the road to hell is paved with good intentions.

Ioana-Iulia Cazacu: I think we previously discussed this as well, but I like to call it designing with empathy and compassion because I think if you try to feel what your audience feels, you can better understand what is and isn't an ethical choice. For me this goes beyond just making people click on one thing over the other or convincing them to make a purchase. It's about how the game intervenes in their relationships when they play together or alone. A drastic example would be someone who is addicted to gambling. That is the kind of thing that affects not only the person but the people around them. I think unethical choices in design propagate and there is a thin line between searching virality for the purpose of the game community and searching virality only for financial gain. In all of this, like you said, the answer is always to question everything and admit that you might be doing things out of habit that are actually not that considerate, but it's hard to admit for sure. And I also think that because what we do is "solve problems" it's very important how we pose the question, what "problem" are we solving and how does that affect the player on a more macro scale.

Patricia Margarit Castelló: Phrasing the problem right as you mentioned is crucial, something we talk continuously about in Fairphone. On one hand, we want to sell phones. We need to in order to be successful and prove our mission, which is to inspire the industry to act more responsibly. But on the other hand, one of our main goals is to decrease e-waste. So if you think about it, our goals may seem to be contradicting themselves. However, like with anything, there is a balance and it's an interesting problem to solve. It comes back to being honest. You can boost people's behaviour and convince them to purchase your product out of all other options, but also properly inform them and encourage them to keep their current phones for longer.

Ioana-Iulia Cazacu: It's important that we think of things beyond just profit when making things that can influence someone psychologically. Obviously you come at this specifically from a point of a company promoting an ethical practice, but I think we could apply this more generally. How do you think this mentality of staying humble, staying honest and doing your research applies to something like, let's say, a more commercial game?

Patricia Margarit Castelló: In my mind it's a bit like this: I'm the creator, I have this idea and I'm creating something I think people are going to like. The key words there are "something *I* think" people will like. It can never not be biased and to me it is super important to be aware of that. Just because you are the one creating it doesn't mean you know everything, and so spending time to learn what people actually want is important. This applies to UX, applies to mechanics and applies to everything. You're a person with ideas and thoughts so of course you will never be truly objective, and you actually should not be. I firmly believe that design should have honest dialogue between creator and audience. That creates a better result than if you didn't have that conversation.

At the beginning of any design work, I find it super important to research the pain points of people in your target audience and get to know their desires. It might sound like a very practical approach to entertainment, but to me this part is crucial. If you think you know best what people want, you will never reach the full potential with your game.

And there is also another side to this: not all games have to be saying something super philosophical, but making a statement with your game adds welcomed complexity. Let's imagine I am making a farming and cooking game where planting produce and making new recipes are the only things you could do. That's valid if that's your goal, but it could lead to a mediocre game, whilst if you do your research and reflect a bit more you may find more layers to add that could potentially make it more interesting.

I think that in this industry, we tend to overlook research and consider it a waste of time. A lot of people have an idea and start creating right away, and I think part of pre-production should really be about understanding the message you want to put across and why. I don't want to say this is the most important phase, but I would say it should be seen as equally as important and taken seriously, not rushing through it.

Ioana-Iulia Cazacu: I agree and despite what people might think, research ends up saving you time when done well. Because it helps you to make better choices or as you said helps you develop your idea in a way that makes it both more complex and more considerate of your audience's preferences.

Patricia Margarit Castelló: Exactly, research gives you the data that allows you to make good decisions.

Ioana-Iulia Cazacu: Precisely that. And I find it interesting when you talk about how research that starts out of concern for ethics has the side effect of making the subject matter more complex, and I agree fully. I'm a big fan of layered design where something is very simple on the surface, but the more you look the deeper it goes. And with your farming game example my mind went straight to *Stardew Valley*. On the surface it's simple: you have your town, you have your farm. But beyond it there is intrigue between the characters, there is commentary about capitalism and how it is destroying the small business balanced out with commentary on how the guy who has the farm shop is the richest guy in town and the more you offer him business the richer he gets. These are interesting real-life topics layered on top of something inconspicuously simple, but it makes that game stand out to me. So like you said it's not that all games must do this, but when they do they are so much more memorable.

Patricia Margarit Castelló: Yes, exactly. *Stardew Valley* is a good example because there are many other farming games which are not as engaging or complex. Some people think it became popular because it was like a new *Harvest Moon*, but there were many other farming games that people would play for a while and then just leave. However, this one is different because of all those layers that you mentioned, because it's not just another farming game. Of course, if you want to play it to relax as a simple farming game, you can, but if you want to dive deeper there are so many different topics to discover, like you just mentioned.

I'm pretty sure it came as a result of the creator taking time to do his research and really think about what he wanted to convey with this game. I remember in an interview he mentioned having analysed a lot of games and adding the things that he would have liked to have but were not there in the other games to *Stardew Valley*.

Ioana-Iulia Cazacu: I suppose that is also kinda going back to our conversation about how games for change can still be fun and engaging. I guess this is one step further that games don't have to be labelled as serious games in order to put forward a message like this, and in fact games are better when they do this.

Patricia Margarit Castelló: Yes, and I think that's kinda the point, that messages are better heard through the metaphor of the game. Because as humans we don't really like being told what to do and how to think. Usually the best way to boost behaviours is to prime them and suggest something when they are open to receiving it.

Something super important that you mentioned earlier and I fully agree with though is that not every game needs to try to teach you something in a very overt way. I think it's more about the subtle little things that make the game feel more "real" and relevant. Adding this to a game is a very delicate craft because you need to do it with a lot of care in order to actually make it work.

Ioana-Iulia Cazacu: I think that is the balance we spoke about between giving people what they want and putting across your own thoughts in a way that is respectful and considerate. I think the best way to present such is to phrase them in a way that allows the audience to decide if something is good or bad. Of course not everything falls in the category of morally debatable though so use your judgement.

Patricia Margarit Castelló: Absolutely. That is what I did with those "protest" games, especially the one I created in Austria. I was an outsider, I just lived there for one year, so while I had my thoughts about the value of preserving a monument such as that bridge, it was not really my place to decide. So I did not want to position myself one way or the other. Instead I tried to learn and understand more about both points of view, because public opinion was divided. The game that resulted was a way for people to be informed about the topic and make up their minds about it in a way that was more engaging than just reading an article, but it was neutral, I did not say this is good or this is bad.

Ioana-Iulia Cazacu: Of course and I think, even if you are at the heart of the issue, it's always important to still try to separate yourself from it when presenting the topic to an audience. And that does not mean having no opinion about it, it does not even mean that the "learnings" of the game don't lean one way or the other. It just means putting in the work of understanding all sides of an argument and presenting them all as a full complex issue, so we are fostering a place where discovery and conversations can happen.

Patricia Margarit Castelló: I fully agree, and something you mentioned that I think is especially important: creating room for debate and discussion. That's what I noticed first-hand with that game I created in Austria. At the end of the game, people that gathered to play it started discussing the topic with each other. I found this super interesting because this was technically not part of the game, but the game was what prompted it so maybe it was part of the game in a greater sense.

Ioana-Iulia Cazacu: That's I think the kind of effect games have on people. We like to talk about games and how they emotionally impact us. That's why they're the perfect medium for social commentary like this because the interaction makes you part of the "issue" and it gets you involved quite literally. Something I found particularly interesting about your project was the social aspect of it, the fact that it was something to be played with others on such a large scale as well. I was hoping you could tell us more about your thought process behind designing an experience like this for a group of people as opposed to designing for an individual experience.

Patricia Margarit Castelló: It is indeed quite different to design for a group playing together than it is designing for one person only. Being in a physical space and playing with a lot of people at the same time presents different challenges. To give an example, when we started designing the game for El Cabanyal in Valencia, we loved the idea of having hundreds of people together, physically in the same space to represent the idea of gathering in a protest. So then the question became "How can we design this game in a way that hundreds of people potentially can play together at the same time?" The answer was obviously not regular controls because that would be not scalable. In the end the solution we went for was the sound interface, which was perfect for the pro-test metaphor, as the players needed to raise their voices or make noise (or not) in order to play.

Then of course, it was all about who was part of our audi-ence and how to present the issue in a way that resonated, where was the best place to get people to play together and how. What I learned during this process was to not generalise. That's some-thing important to keep in mind, that even though you are addressing a group you must not assume that this group is homo-geneous, because you will not get to reach them. Instead, treat the topic in a complex way like we discussed earlier.

Ioana-Iulia Cazacu: That makes complete sense of course and some-thing that crossed my mind as you were talking about this was "accessibility" and "approachability". Something like the sound interface assumes no prior knowledge of games; everyone can use their voice or their body to make noise. I think this is another thing with serious games and social games in different ways. Something that is meant to be easily understood and engaged with by multiple people with varying levels of understanding of games, interest and ability.

Patricia Margarit Castelló: Exactly. To me, ethics and accessibility are related, and there are three key pillars: accessibility, diversity and inclusivity. These are not always taken into account when designing games, but they are very important if you want to cre-ate games in an ethical way. Of course, it depends on the game and the target audience, but it's a good practice to consider them as much as possible.

Ioana-Iulia Cazacu: This was a wonderful interview. Thank you for your time and your amazing insight. As a final question, is there something you would like to highlight and for people to take on from our conversation?

Patricia Margarit Castelló: I cannot stress enough the need to do this research with an open mind in order to not misinterpret the data. When you are researching something that you already have a bias of, you run the risk of just manipulating this data without being aware of it. It's not easy to distance yourself, but it's vital for creating an ethical product. Remaining honest and humble when it comes to what you know and what you don't know as a designer.

Another recommendation is to always be respectful of the user's feelings, because in the end feelings matter a lot, and be aware of the tiny things that sneak up on you and have a big impact, bigger than you might not realise. Something as simple as changing a word can make a huge difference.

And last but not least, thanks so much for this amazing interview. It's been great to discuss these topics with you. I appreciate your time and insights too.

Notes

1. I would encourage reading the article "Is Video Game Addiction Really an Addiction?" by Mark Zastrow in the journal *Proceedings of the National Academy of Sciences* to discover more.
2. This is true of *Coin Master* as of November 2023, when the analysis was made.
3. See Johan Huizinga, *Homo Ludens ILS 86*, Taylor & Francis Group, 2014.

Part 4

Innovative game design

chapter 10

From observation to innovation

We hear a lot of talk about innovation in terms of business strategy, those glittery conferences for tech startups where people focus predominantly on finding what is the very next thing to work on. If you are interested in knowing more about the world of business innovation there are many publications that will satisfy that need to know the best ways to foster innovation in a team as a leader.

But as a designer who worked for a while on innovative solutions for unique problems I have to say I found there is not enough granularity to help with the day-to-day task of innovative thinking rather than the overall strategy of it. Sometimes even when all "conditions are met" and we have the best shot at innovating, the individual must still manage their own creative process and be aware of what is the best way to approach the problems at hand. I am also not of the belief that some people are more prone to innovation than others necessarily. If you have an interest in innovation and the skills to do the job, you are already most of the way there. While I don't think there is a straight road or trick to this kind of thinking, there are techniques that help you get closer to the desired result, and with time the more you apply this structure the more natural it becomes.

Here are some of the methods that I have learned or created in order to keep myself on track and honest.

Innovation starts with observation

In order to be able to improve something you need to first understand it as well as possible. This is the first principle of design in any situation. But beyond the concept of understanding the problem at hand and how to use existing methods to solve it, thinking innovatively is about expanding what you are looking at for inspiration and maybe searching for answers in "unlikely places". In my opinion an almost surefire way to stagnate is to only consider your field of expertise when looking for creative solutions, and if we listen to interviews with established figures in the games industry we know that more often than not interesting ideas come from unexpected places.

Some of these "answers" are going to be happenstance, where something happens around us that will incite us to think of a solution we have not considered before. However, we cannot rely on inspiration to strike, we

DOI: 10.1201/9781003314325-14

need to be proactive. Part of the skill of pushing something forward consistently is knowing how wide to cast your net when doing research. It has to be wide enough in order to get those "unexpected" sources to appear, but not so wide that it will become confusing or use up a lot of time.

No personal knowledge is truly irrelevant

When sitting down to solve a problem as a designer you bring with you the wealth of knowledge you have acquired over the years. Especially when talking about game design I really do believe no past information is truly irrelevant; understanding the world in all of its facets is very important. A good amount of general knowledge will make us not only more sympathetic to the experience of other people, but it will also give us a wealth of tools to approach a problem. This is why personal development is so important and especially personal development that extends beyond the boundaries of the immediate game design sphere. Fields like human psychology, product design or film have a wealth of resources for us to use and apply to the games we make (especially given the fact they are all established academic fields that are older than game theory).

But there is no reason to limit ourselves only to the "immediately relevant" when building our internal knowledge library because the truth is we never really know how information can spark an idea. Obviously accumulating knowledge takes time, but I think having a mindset where all information passing through our brains could eventually be used in a creative process that truly changes the way we approach things.

More often than not we see the "immediate relevance" of a subject matter being brought up as a critique of educational curriculum everywhere, but the truth of the matter is that we as humans choose if we use the information given to us. Instead of discarding things as not immediately relevant, storing them to use for later and searching for opportunities to apply that stored knowledge is what we should be aiming for. Obviously there will never be a way for us to use everything we know, just as there will never be a way to know everything there is to know. But embracing knowledge of all kinds means that when we sit down to design something we consider a wealth of knowledge that we already have and as a result we can make connections we wouldn't be able to make otherwise.

Involved and informed

In my experience it pays to be informed of the things that happen in your area of expertise and the immediate adjacent area (for example, games should always pay attention to at least tech and film). Beyond just paying attention to specialty publications it is also a great advantage if you can directly interact with others who are innovating by joining spaces where such things are discussed. This might not give you a super detailed view of what others are doing, but it would give you the information earlier and help you understand where the product you are working on can position itself on the market. More often than not, conferences are a great place to chat with others about what they are doing, and this should help you keep your mind open to what's on the horizon.

When talking to other people who are innovating, the goal should not be to scout out what will happen in the future as that is impossible to predict. The goal is to look at their findings and see if they are relevant to us in some way. The research other people are doing and their preliminary findings can help us ask different questions, reconsider a "truth" that we have taken for granted or even adjust course if we think it is necessary. Obviously we have to be able to trust the validity of what people say, so there is more to this than just hearing an anecdote and changing your design thinking. Instead use these findings as starting points for further explorations, maybe further experiments to run in your own product.

Know your history

It is not enough to understand the current state of your topic of interest, as what we see right now is the product of iteration over time. The history of a product or a field tells you a lot about what has been tried and what the results were. Having a good grasp of video game history in general is important, as is understanding how we have come to certain conclusions, why the medium is the way that it is and why we are using certain design devices over others. This I believe should be part of the designer's general knowledge library ready to access. The more targeted historical research is reserved for the moments just before embarking on the journey of developing a game. Ask yourself the following questions and research in order to answer them to the best of your ability:

1. Did others try something like this before?
2. If others did try, how did it go?
3. If others didn't try, what prevented them from doing so?
4. If similar products were unsuccessful, why was that?
5. If similar products were successful, what generated that success?
6. If predecessors have a success and downfall story, what caused their downfall?

These questions allow you to position the product you are working on in the larger picture of things coming and going. Very rarely is an idea truly unique. Chances are if you dig enough you will find people talking about the same ideas you had at some point in the past. Sometimes technology isn't advanced enough to realise an idea or society isn't quite ready to embrace it. Sometimes it all works out brilliantly for a while until circumstances change and it all crashes and burns. Learning from what has been tried before will not only allow you to answer questions about your own work, but it will hopefully make you learn from other people's experiences.

It is also important to have a good understanding of your own product history. This is because when making a step to improve something you need to understand what direction it was moving into and what value already existing users get out of it. Ask yourself:

1. What was the initial idea for this product and how does it compare to what we have so far?
2. If the game is live, what does the data look like and what kind of experiments were run in the past? What has worked and what hasn't?
3. What is the latest user feedback? What have we previously user-tested and what have we learned from those tests?
4. What are historically the main key performance indicator struggles for this game?

It is important to look beyond the surface when looking at history and understand the whys that make the games you are looking at what they are. It is easy to ascribe value to popular things, justifying that if they were popular they must have done it right. Or just the same it's easy to hold on to hope that if a "failing" game had a small incredibly devoted following, marketing would have been the solution to make it "successful". The reality is always more complex than the "facts" of a game's performance, and this is why understanding the circumstances is the most important part of research because nothing happens in isolation. While being informed does not mean you are impervious to the unpredictable nature of the future, it does mean that you can give yourself the best chance at making the right decisions when the time comes.

Innovate in the areas you care about

When making something that is meant to be innovative there is a strong temptation to overdesign everything and search for the most ingenious solutions in every single aspect of the game. While in theory this will lead to the most unique design, there is a roster of reasons why this way of thinking is unlikely to work in your favour.

First, we have to take into consideration time as a real-world barrier to what we can achieve. If we refuse to take any shortcuts in design and never rely on the things that have been proven and set up before us, we risk sinking a lot of money and effort into things that are not immediately related to the innovation we want our product to bring to the market.

Think, for example, of the standard settings menu. We could in theory come up with a "better", more intuitive user experience (UX) design for this type of menu, but at the end of the day how important is this menu for the player? How often is the player interacting with it, and is the time spent to improve it going to result in increased interest on the player's part? This is why it is incredibly important to know exactly what it is that makes your game unique, the goal you are trying to achieve and to make sure that all the time is spent on improving the things that will inch you closer to that goal. Usually strong game direction will cover questions regarding "what you are trying to achieve and what you should be working on. But even in the day-to-day design decisions, there is plenty of room to consider what innovation brings true value and what innovation would be a waste of time.

Secondly, we have to consider familiarity bias, which suggests that people are more likely to prefer something that feels already familiar. Things unfamiliar to the player are not rejected but rather they require more time and cognitive effort from the player. This is why it is better to sprinkle unique ideas among others more familiar to make sure players are not overwhelmed trying to understand all the different new concepts presented to them. In my experience players need to be primed by the game to accept the innovative ideas it brings forward, otherwise the answer is most commonly confusion and frustration, which can lead to players quitting the game (remember the involvement meter). Priming the player is all about matching player expectations that are built either through the game's positioning on the market or through the previous interaction they had with the game. If the player knows the unique selling points of the game and they are eased by the user experience into encountering these unique elements, the player will likely be better prepared to put in the effort it takes to understand the innovative elements.

Thirdly, we know humans remember things that are unique and unexpected more than they do commonplace things; it's a way for our brains to keep them. Having too many novel ideas in the same experience takes away from the experience of encountering something new. Think about it as the cherry on top of the sundae; it's special because it is unique. These moments of novelty can be used as pick-me-ups to increase the player's excitement and involvement in the game. This it's why my personal preference is to make sure unique experiences are evenly distributed, especially during the first-time user experience. This ensures each of these features has the opportunity to be acknowledged and understood, but it also means that they can be used to excite the player after you had them go through some less exciting but necessary parts.

Being able to innovate where it counts is all about understanding your own product, always making decisions to support the core tenets of your game and making sure that every decision contributes to the ultimate goal of the game

Don't get in your own way

One of the most frequent struggles in innovative design is not being able to break through the box that we build ourselves. More often than not we fall prey to the same familiarity bias that players do: we prefer methods we have seen and used in the past instinctually and something without giving it much thought. While using universal design language can make something more intuitive by virtue of being what people are already used to, sometimes creative answers can offer us an opportunity to solve something in a more suitable way for our audience. And it goes beyond just ourselves. When working in a team we can get influenced by the opinions of those around us and play safer than we should in a desire to please everyone. While there is no flawless way to fully eliminate these kinds of barriers and biases, there are methods that can be employed to keep ourselves honest and keep pushing ourselves to be creative.

Involve non-developers

The early stage of ideation is when you can fully let your imagination run wild. This stage is cheap and therefore entertaining really out-there ideas is perfectly justifiable as long as the ideation process is kept within a reasonable time frame. This is a great moment to involve everyone, especially people on the team who might not typically get involved with design or even just development work in general. What I have found is that often those who do not do this kind of work every day have an easier time suggesting ideas that are out-there, and while there is definitely some work that will go into exploring those ideas and sifting out what is not really suitable this can sometimes bring to the table very interesting concepts.

In design we often hear that ideas are "cheap" and that everyone can have ideas. I do think this is true and this is exactly something that can be leveraged to our advantage. Some people might not have the know-how to turn an idea into a design, they might not even have the ability to fully formulate their ideas and that is where I think the work of a good designer shines. In the end our job is not to be the originators of any specific idea, instead it is to be the connective tissue that connects all the ideas into a good cohesive product.

Using "yes, and" in game design

A concept that originates from improv is the concept of responding with "yes, and" to what others say and letting ideas grow in directions you might not have expected them to. I was first introduced to the concept of "yes, and" in the context of tabletop role-playing games. There the same concept is applied by the game master in order to offer players enough freedom to impact the world, so the resulting events feel like a collaboration between the game master's plot and the player's solutions. And it is because of this specific experience with role-playing games that I thought about using this technique in my game design exploration.

Be it in collaborative design or solo work, using "yes, and" can yield very interesting results because it allows you to unlock your mind and explore beyond the usual. This technique can be very helpful especially when you are feeling a bit of a creative block when the usual solutions seem to not give the right results. The aim is not to get a perfect string of cohesive ideas but rather to see where the path takes you and if any of the steps on the path are something you would like to explore further in your game. It also makes collaboration with others a lot easier, ensuring no ideas are shut down before given a proper chance to prove their worth.

Understand trends before following them

Video games, much like other forms of entertainment, tend to go through cycles of content being "popular" most commonly following the advent of a specific game becoming very popular or the introduction of new technology. These trends oftentimes extend beyond themes and genres, and down into the nitty gritty of game design. This incorporation of popular mechanics into more and more games does not have to happen on purpose (although some people are deliberate about it), but it is worth remembering that as creatives we draw our inspiration from the things around us, and we might not even be 100% aware.

Because of this assimilation of mechanics that happens partially organically I believe it is best to be intentional about adopting any of those popular mechanics into your game. Really consider the benefits and the problems that it brings along with it and why it is popular in the first place. Being intentional about something like this means that ultimately we do not fall prey to following a trend that by the time we might put the game out it would be already gone. Instead we consider our goals and how mechanics can facilitate us reaching them.

Invisible innovation

Innovation does not have to be obvious to make a huge difference to the overall product. Oftentimes it is the little steps we take toward solving problems where most of the creative design can lie. This is not the kind of innovation that will get you any kind of statue built in your honour but it is in my opinion what pushes the whole industry further, slowly, imperceptibly but always on the move. I call this invisible innovation because it is not so much about people being aware that you are trying to give them a new solution to something but rather challenging the existing patterns of design and making it so that the overall experience is so much better than it would have been without it.

Invisible innovation is what ultimately derives from iteration and is something that happens every day in games development by the very nature of how we do things. I believe it is interesting to talk about it in isolation because this kind of innovation is usually not given enough space to shine, although it is the fundamental building block of design in general: "creatively solving small problems in a better way than they have been solved before".

Part of this is being aware of current design patterns and breaking them on purpose in order to get the player's attention. The "familiar" is both a tool and a trick when it comes to design. As discussed earlier, we tend to like familiar things, we know how to use a familiar tool and there is societal knowledge of what certain things look and behave like. In many cases familiar design is a shortcut to get the user through the stuff that they don't need to think about and instead to get them to engage with something that we consider to be more important.

Sometimes, however, the exact same effect that can be used positively in this way will make players skip over content that we as designers would rather they did not skip. A great example of such an instance is players' reactions to tutorials. I would say that throughout time, tutorials have been much improved in content and how they go about teaching players what they need to do. That being said players' expectations of tutorials have not improved over the years and most commonly people tend to skip this content if they can, rendering the improvement to the content useless. Because users have become accustomed to skipping tutorials they will keep doing so no matter how useful that tutorial might be. And they will do so even to their detriment because the decision to skip it is not something the player does after careful consideration of the tutorial's benefits but rather something they block automatically. In cognitive psychology this is called System 1 thinking, and it comprises all the actions that the user does on impulse, even if that "instinct" stems from a learned behaviour over time.[1]

This kind of thinking is great at making sure our brains don't get overwhelmed by the vast amounts of information available in the world. It filters out things that are unrelated to what we are trying to achieve, redundant in general or even too high of an effort to process. The tutorial example then falls into two of these three abovementioned categories: they are higher effort to process because learning is high effort and they have been historically considered not of interest. Because of this effect we as developers must convince the players' brains that the content is worth their time and the effort to parse. This is most commonly done by challenging existing design and breaking the pattern so players can get over their initial reaction.

This is where what I call "invisible innovation" comes in: the art of presenting something old in a new way and getting the player to pay attention more than they would' otherwise. To do this there are a few main ways to circumvent System 1 thinking and get the player to be more involved:

- **Making the content approachable**: Anything that looks intimidating at a point where the player is not yet ready to receive that content is basically a write-off.
- **Increase the involvement meter to prep the user**: Previously we discussed how users are more or less ready to "understand" what is happening based on how involved they are. Timing is then essential to introducing new things to the player. Things have to be appropriately complex and spaced out in order to keep them involved.
- **Break the mould, surprise and delight:** Here is where invisible innovation comes into play. You want to approach things in a new way that surprises the player and delights them with the interaction so they are more likely to pay attention.

While the delight of the innovator comes to a certain degree from the very nature of the discovery, that is ultimately not the final point of innovation. Instead we are working towards uncovering the next steps in the overall evolution of the products we are working on be they a physical object or a piece of entertainment software. Innovation is there to ease the experience of those using what we make to make their lives easier or better in some way.[2] Our aim is not to reinvent the wheel but to give the user the best wheel experience they have had so far by using innovation subtly and in the right places.

Innovation and design: Interview with Matthew Wiggins

Matthew Wiggins and I have been working together for many years, exploring in detail the intricacies of designing for a group of people. His drive for innovation and history of exploring uncharted territories in the world of entertainment and tech make him a treasure trove of knowledge when it comes to how the process can be improved. In this interview Matthew and I talk a bit about the importance of aiming to innovate but we also talk about the history of social games and how we build upon what had come before in a smart way.

Matthew Wiggins: Hello, my name is Matthew Wiggins. I'm the CEO of Mojiworks. I've been in the tech industry since the 2000s, originally as a programmer and designer in the games industry. I also led teams in the games industry and other consumer tech industries, like 3D printing, AR [augmented reality] and other technologies, but always focused on consumer products. And from running teams is how I got to building companies.

I became interested in computers when I was about five years old because I grew up in the '80s and was fortunate enough to be exposed to computers and tech at a time when it was a really unusual niche. I was not only interested in tech, but I was also into a lot of other things. Initially I went to university to study mechanical engineering because I wanted to design racing cars. And whilst I was there, my best friend was doing a sandwich year working for a games company. They needed help with some physics calculations in the game so I went to help them out, and I never went back to university. I didn't drop out to actually work for that company, but because I knew that I wanted to get into the tech industry rather than engineering. And I spent long enough at university by that point that I couldn't afford to stay and I needed to leave if I wasn't gonna finish it. I worked for a telecoms company for a bit, and then I got my first job in the games industry.

Since then I've started companies, I've sold companies, done a lot of different things and probably I would say that the reason why I've been able to do quite a lot of interesting things is because of being able to communicate and care deeply about people.

Ioana-Iulia Cazacu: You mentioned the different types of tech you have been in throughout the years, and since you do tend to go into these quite cutting-edge fields I was wondering what is the pull towards innovation for you?

Matthew Wiggins: I am really interested in creating things and obviously that's inherently about making something new. But new tech is also an interesting problem to solve. That's exactly what technology is about, almost literally that's with the word means. So I'm puzzled when people who work or invest in technology seem to sort of reject that. The way I see it is that discovery is just something that will naturally happen. So the question becomes "Can we accelerate discovery?" And I think that's a good thing to do because those discoveries are always gonna happen at some point with or without you. So let's try and do them as early as possible because new findings can always be used in a range of different ways. Some of which you might deem as positive, some of which are negative, particularly from a cultural point of view. That's always gonna happen.

A great example is understanding the atom and nuclear fission. There is a lot of good and bad you can do with that, but what an interesting thing to know about, right? One of my all-time heroes is a guy called Richard Feynman, who was a physicist and polymath in the 20th century. And one of his great books (and actually a TV program) is called *The Pleasure of Finding Things Out.*[3] And I completely believe in that joy of just discovering things.

My point is, new things will always be discovered, but we decide how to use them. That's the really interesting thing to me, because you can't stop technology. So coming back to the example with nuclear fission: on one side you can figure out a way of generating unlimited clean power, and on the other you can destroy the world. It's up to us what we do with it. For me, that is what is so exciting about innovation. I'm not very interested in regurgitating stuff. I'd much rather try the new thing that doesn't work to find out that it doesn't than work on something that I know is already going to work, but is basically the same thing again.

Ioana-Iulia Cazacu: Sort of related to your personal history then, I was wondering if you can tell me more about your experiences of playing games with other people.

Matthew Wiggins: The very first experience playing games with people was actually playing solo games while being with others, in the very early '80s. When I was maybe five years old (about 1985), The Nintendo Game & Watch (those things are awesome) and we would actually just pass them around mainly from some rich kid that had a Game & Watch and would show it off. Everyone would come to them like "Can I have a go? Can I have a go?" The other thing would be playing *Pong.* So although this is slightly before my time, the Binatone TV Master. It was basically analogue *Pong* home consoles that you plug into the back of the TV. I actually still have one, they're pretty awesome. You've got two little paddles and just a rotary control on them. That's probably the very first time playing a video game with somebody else for me.

We would play a lot of solo games when friends would come over. Mostly we would take turns to play and watch. I remember one of the best Christmases was in 1990 when I got a Game Boy. It was my dream to get one and Mom actually did an awesome job of hiding what it was in the runup to Christmas, so I ran over to the box under the tree and it was too big and when I shook it, it rattled, so I was sure I wasn't getting it that year. Come Christmas day, I open the box and inside is the Game Boy box, with some bits of wood kindling from our fire. Tetris was the only game on it but my birthday is in January only a couple of weeks after Christmas. So for my birthday I got *Super Mario Land,* and Al, who's my best friend (and my cofounder), came over with a few other friends for a small birthday celebration which we basically spent playing *Super Mario Land* passing the Game Boy around. And of course it was my birthday, my Game Boy and we got to a particular point where you get an extra life and on the next screen there's an opportunity to die and I just kept dying at this point kinda in an infinite loop. And this went on for a while but to me it didn't feel that long, but I am sure my friends didn't see it that way. That is a very vivid memory to me.

In later years when it really became a thing to actually play games together, we would have LAN parties. For a variety of reasons, Al his family has like a couple of different computers so we hook those up and play *Doom*, multiplayer. That was a "Holy shit!" moment because we did all of this stuff at a time when this was really niche. Mainstream culture basically looked down on someone like Bill Gates and he got ridiculed when he said in the early '80s that "every desk and every home" is going to have a computer. Everyone was thinking "This guy's an idiot, why would you need that?" So that feeling of hooking to computers together and playing *Doom* amazed me. This was somewhere in "94 maybe. In the '90s, there was this kind of explosion of being able to play these relatively high-fidelity games together.

The other one, of course, would be arcades in the late '80s. I remember playing *Gauntlet*, a four-player cooperative real-time game. My dad had taken me swimming and there was an arcade machine there and I was obsessed with games, so of course I put my pocket money into this game which was properly full on (in some ways similar to *Vampire Survivors* but made in 1985). My dad didn't think I was playing it, he thought I was just watching it and said we had to go, trying to pull me away from this machine while I was trying to hold back tears because I was right in the middle of playing this thing with somebody else. That game had a good mix of cooperative while also trying to be better than each other, and that is another one of my vivid memories.

Ioana-Iulia Cazacu: This is my favourite question to ask because I think it positions games as always being kind and social, even when playing "together" is not possible. Obviously now we have multiplayer and games that we actually call "social", but play I think is universally a bonding activity. Following on from that, can you tell us more about your own history with social games, specifically in the Facebook era and beyond, maybe tell us about how the idea for hyper-social started?

Matthew Wiggins: I started a games company in 2009 that was all about making games for the iPhone. It was the first company that

I started and the idea for it was triggered by Apple creating the App Store for the iPhone ecosystem (which many people don't remember, it wasn't there to begin with). The iPhone was really interesting creatively, but it also created some new and exciting business opportunities. The company we started was going to be a one-game company, and our aim was to make a particular game (the game is irrelevant for the purpose of this because that was just a solo game). At the time we were working with this publisher and they were based in San Francisco, and this was at the same time when Zynga was doing Facebook games. I knew about Zynga because I've been on one of their GDC [Game Developers Conference] talks, probably in 2009 a few months before I started this first company. Ngmoco, who was the publisher we were working with at the time, were doing a game inspired by Facebook games not too dissimilar to *FarmVille* with a different development team. It was called *We Rule* and it's made by the people that ended up making *Words with Friends*. That was the first time I interacted with anything like a social game, though they were not known by that name yet.

We ended up selling that first company to Zynga because at the time they were big on Facebook, but they wanted to get big on mobile and we were relatively big on mobile, so they bought us. They also bought that company that made *Words with Friends* and we all became part of Zynga. That is when I really started seeing social games from the inside, which was this really interesting experience of understanding how embedded in the platform they are (it's right in their name!). Zynga's whole idea in the beginning was to use Facebook as a platform for games; they weren't trying to become their own platform. Fast forward six to seven years later, and by that time social games had settled down a bit, Facebook wasn't such a big games platform anymore and most stuff had shifted to mobile. At the time I was advising a company, they were a business-to-business chat app that unexpectedly came to be used for some games stuff in the Middle East, where the users were contriving games like *Werewolf* and similar kinds of stuff on this platform. I thought it was interesting but I didn't know where that could really go. At the time (mid-2010s) VR [virtual reality] had the games industry and the tech industry concerned but I was super sceptical about it because I remember being a kid in the early '90s as VR was going to be the next big thing then. And it was pretty awesome, but only for about five minutes and if you're 13, but it didn't go anywhere. So

I was not interested in VR, but I was looking for what the next thing might be as I always tend to do. I was actually working on some AR stuff and I was at WWDC 2016 [Worldwide Developers Conference]. And as a real throwaway thing, they announced that there was gonna be an App Store in iMessage. On my way back from America I ended up talking to someone, who was also at WWDC, and I thought this iMessage store could be interesting, you could put games there. And she wasn't a game developer but she thought that was a really interesting idea. So I came back and I started Mojiworks.

I like taking the plunge. I really believe that perfection is the enemy of good. I think some people don't want to do things until they have been "proven", but of course by the time everything is settled the opportunity has already gone because someone else has already done it. And like with anything there are risks, one being that you are so heavily influenced by the platform of course, but to a degree you see this with consoles and storefronts of all kinds. There are many great games on consoles virtually nobody owns anymore. And obviously with all these new platforms that open up the opportunity for games, the question is "What does a great game on this platform look like?" and that is where the social game 2.0 came, or hyper-social.

Ioana-Iulia Cazacu: And Facebook games as they used to be pretty much exited the arena which leaves a bit of a gap for those who want to play socially in that light way.

Matthew Wiggins: Games on Facebook are actually still a really big deal but for a completely different audience now, which is the social casino audience. If you look at Zynga's financial results, they are still making loads of money from social casino games on Facebook. They are really good at finding and captivating the non-gaming audience, middle-aged and older. Most of those people did not grow up with games and they even grew up in a society that frowned upon games unless you were a kid. Being a teen in the '90s was the era of games as "murder simulators, rotting, the brains of our children" basically all you hear about social media now. History doesn't repeat but it does rhyme. You see these things happening in cycles.

So for me I am wondering "What can we learn from Zynga and Facebook?" We know people love playing games together, so giving a mainstream audience a way of playing games together in a place where they're already hanging out makes sense. But we are trying to discover what's the right platform or platforms for this next generation of social games. Because the old ones basically died, but they didn't die because they were bad. They died because another technology came along and the design was no longer suited for the way our lives are now, post the advent of smartphones in every pocket and taking the internet wherever we go.

Ioana-Iulia Cazacu: I think it's also about the audience. We noticed that our audience is not only tech savvy but they are very aware of how to socially interact online. They craft their identity online; they will not be bamboozled into sharing stuff they don't want on their feed. You would not be able even if you wanted to to pull the wool over their eyes and convince them to do something that they don't want to do. With Gen Z even trying something like that can make you very much disliked. And it's not that earlier on we didn't know, although I am sure some of us really didn't understand the extent of it, but it was all a little more exciting and unregulated. For Gen Z being online is commonplace and I think they just treat it differently.

Matthew Wiggins: Yes and that's why you can't regurgitate all that stuff just on a new platform. There is so much choice, so a low-quality rip-off would not do it. Because they are already used to communicating while playing existing games, people used Discord for that all the time. Instead these games should give you the opportunity to play something that you can only be on that platform and is enabled by it. Our audience is a very clued-up, savvy, game-literate audience partly because of their age quite frankly. So what can we give them on a platform they use that will mean they get an experience they could not have somewhere else already? It will come as no surprise to you that for what we are doing I believe the answer to be: social.

Ioana-Iulia Cazacu: Talking about social as a pillar of the work we do, I was wondering if you had other pillars when you started out with the company. I guess another way of putting it is how you approached innovation in that sense.

Matthew Wiggins: I guess we decided not to do something obvious with it, that was the first thing. We looked at iMessage and what we decided was the obvious thing to do was a word game, because turn-based seemed to be the thing for it because it mimicked the way you were sending messages. So, we zeroed in on asynchronous but definitely not making a word game. I think one of the first actual pillars was that we wanted to learn very quickly, that was a lesson I carried over from previous companies. It's much more valuable to learn than it is to try and do something that you think is gonna be perfect, especially in an uncharted area like this because you are just making a guess. Something about innovation is that you can't really look at other people and see what they have already done and copy that. It's what really makes something like this hard. You have to discover things as you go and do it quickly. As a startup VCs [venture capitalists] actually don't really want the innovators, because there's a saying that pioneers get shot in the back.

Ioana-Iulia Cazacu: Obviously that is kinda what happened to the social games, because none of the big Zynga games were their original ideas.

Matthew Wiggins: Exactly! So that is why it's fundamental to be experimental to learn quickly. And for social games you have a double problem to solve. Making products for one person is difficult enough, but what will a group of people like when they are trying to spend time together, that was our main question.

So our second pillar was really obvious, which is like we wanted these games to be really social. The whole point of them was that you were playing with friends. We wanted these games to facilitate the relationships already existing between people.

A third pillar was to always push the boundaries, which is not the same as trying things out quickly. You can do something fast and not learn very much from it. It kinda goes back to that first decision to not make a word game. And we knew that Zynga would have the ability and desire to do that (a word game) anyway and a lot faster than us, and sure enough they did.

Ioana-Iulia Cazacu: What we do kinda evolved throughout the years as the tech evolved, but obviously iMessage is a messenger and there were previous games on messaging platforms, so I was wondering how much was there to hand onto when you started out?

Matthew Wiggins: Not very much to be honest, even at times I felt like those previous systems looked more similar than they actually were because a lot of them were really synchronous. Stuff like AOL, ICQ and others like that the use case was different. You would sit down and use them in a synchronous kind of way. iMessage was not like that. I was really focused on asynchronous messaging and notifications. My thinking was that games can be asynchronous and played at any time, and it will be like sending little packets backwards and forwards and then we check in with each other throughout the day even if we can't synchronously "chat". That felt very innovative, and it wasn't much you could lean on for that except for maybe play-by-mail, or play-by-email stuff like *Diplomacy*. The goal was to very much fit inside the conversation, and offer these game-play experiences that could be really quick but still rewarding, like sending a message and that helps you keep in touch with someone.

I find that probably marginally more interesting than the real-time stuff from a pure design point of view because it's just really strange and unusual. But that was the core idea for our first game MojiQuest. Another inspiration was *StreetPass Quest*, a Nintendo DS game where you would walk and when you had a moment to check it you would return to a bunch of content related to other people with the game that you passed by. The DS was a really inspirational device for me anyway because it came out right around the time that my child was born and my whole approach to playing games changed. I suddenly no longer had time to sit down and play for hours. I needed something that would fit in with my life, and in the early 2000s the tendency was that games would be more and more heavyweight. I really liked the idea of returning to some of those sorts of values.

Ultimately these people are not on social media to play games; they are there to feel like they are keeping up with their friends. The challenge is to figure out how the experience you are making can fit into someone's life and enhance it.

Ioana-Iulia Cazacu: I believe games kind of didn't transition well when Facebook became mobile, because people didn't use the platform in the same way. When Facebook was primarily used only on the computer, you would sit for a chunk of time "using it". *FarmVille* had long sessions and the game was paced for the platform as it used to be before it transitioned to mobile. There were obviously a lot of platform changes that affected it, but the changing in people's habits is what really killed it I think. And it's not like people don't spend long stretches of time on social media now, they just do it in a more "pick'n'mix" kind of way.

Matthew Wiggins: Something that Zynga was big into and it's not something you hear so much about now was to deliberately limit people's playtime. You can look at the monetisation model from all of those games. The question was how long do we want someone to really play before they leave? The view was (and I think this was correct) that the appointment mechanics were really strong retention drivers. What you wanted people to do, is come in, set up a load of appointments and leave. But you also want to monetise that, right? So the monetisation in *FarmVille* was really driven initially by the energy mechanics. That would also limit your session time but of course, they wanted people to pay for more energy. This fit better for match-three games, for example, in *Candy Crush* it was a bit more natural.

FarmVille was ideal for that long session thing, as you said, we can just sit there kind of like tapping away and cleaning stuff up and then wait 15 minutes for your energy to be back. *Hay Day* is an example of a similar kind of game that was actually designed with mobile as a platform. The amount of time spent in a session is a fascinating topic, and it's especially tricky to get right when the game can be played on multiple platforms. This was true of Facebook games in the early 2010s, but it is also true for us now with platforms like Discord, which are both desktop and mobile.

Ioana-Iulia Cazacu: Absolutely! One of the things that I like analysing (especially since the pandemic) is how people behave socially online in different spaces. Because everything influences your behaviour I think: the design of the platform, the people on there and what voices get amplified and yes even the device we use them on.

Matthew Wiggins: It definitely does. If the platform is successful I think it evolves into a symbiotic relationship between the users and the platform. The platform starts to modify itself to meet the users and users get used to the platform's quirks. You can see all sorts of different platforms going all sorts of different directions. You can see this with all social media and especially in retrospect with the older social platforms. If you think about Myspace, Tumblr, all that stuff, none of them ended up looking quite the same as each other. I think it's like evolution, there's just millions of little things that happen. Twitter is another really good example. Each platform kind of becomes unique in its relationship with the users be that for the better or worse.

Ioana-Iulia Cazacu: This is not to say that there isn't a variety of people on these platforms. This is why I feel quite strongly about just having different layers of interaction in the game for different types of people. It's not about making games that lack complexity, it's more about being able to interact with as much or as little as you want. Making a game a group of friends can use as a conduit for spending time together. I believe this is why simple games are usually good to be played with others, because everyone can "get it", but what if it was a better way to keep everyone together and give them the different levels of interaction they are looking for.

Matthew Wiggins: Yes, and of course that's the difficulty with social games for a mainstream audience; these people are not all the same as each other. The experiments we have done surrounding PvP [player versus player] were really interesting because of the brutalness of a purely adversarial player-to-player interaction. But I think co-op stuff is so much cooler because there is a lot more opportunity to hang out and have fun with people that have different expertise levels and different tastes. I think it's why people talk about couch co-op and lament the fact that it is kinda going away. But the main point is that playing with other people has to make the experience easier to enjoy.

Take for example the new *Super Mario Brothers*; it doesn't really do a great job of co-op in my opinion. When I play it with my wife and daughter there is a huge difference in skill. When somebody dies, they'll float onto the screen in a bubble where they're basically protected until someone bursts them out. But ultimately, they still have to be able to run through a Mario level and that is not easy and the game makes you feel like you are babysitting the others without actually making it easier because you are playing together. If anything, playing with somebody else makes it slightly harder because apart from you pulling them along the screen is zooming out as well.

Ioana-Iulia Cazacu: That is something I believe to be most important ultimately when it comes to making any game that has the goal to bring people together and play. The game has to be accessible for me and those I am friends with. The goal is that the game is truly at its best when it is played socially. It's not a game that I could play by myself and feel like there is no difference. It's definitely a risky move, because not only is it a difficult task to create something like this, but it kinda relies on people having someone to play with. And this is why it's so important that the game fosters a good community and helps people form friendships inside the game as well as accommodating the people who already have a group of friends willing to play.

Matthew Wiggins: I think if there was any lesson to take from this conversation it would be that when you are aiming to design a social game it is fundamental you think not only of the entertainment of the individual player but the entertainment of the group. And this can only be done by observing people's behaviours and catering to their wants and needs as best we can.

Notes

1. Concept popularised by Daniel Kahneman in his book *Thinking Fast and Slow* (2011; Farrar, Straus and Giroux).
2. Consider looking into the wonderful UX design case studies and courses from Growth.Design on Product Design Psychology: https://growth.design /psychology.
3. Feynman, R. P., & Robbins, J. *The Pleasure of Finding Things Out: The Best Short Works of Richard P. Feynman.* (1999; Perseus Books).

Conclusion

From the beginning stages of writing this book I knew there would be a healthy dose of interlacing games theory with my personal experience in the field of social games. During the research however, I truly understood how well the behaviour we were noticing in the audience playing our games mapped to social concepts from academic study both in the field of games and outside of it. At the end of the day design has the ultimate goal of creating things that people use and thus social sciences become fundamental in understanding how to best do so.

Online has been a nebulous territory for many years. The use of it has evolved predominantly organically over time as a dialogue between those making things on the internet and those consuming them. The social quirks and qualities of this environment may at first feel completely alien, but if we analyse things through the lens of human behaviour we start to unravel the motivations behind it all. In this book I have attempted to my best knowledge and ability to interlink my personal lived experience as a developer of social games with research and observed player motivations. This is because I do not believe there is a clear-cut recipe for a perfect social game, instead a game designed with social in mind must first and foremost understand how people express themselves and interact with one another. Social interaction will keep evolving with our means of communication and whatever we make with the intent of playing a part in the way people bond with each other must first and foremost take into consideration how those bonds are being formed in the first place.

In this book I reference this emerging type of game I refer to as hyper-social. I do this with the intention of giving a name to something that has slowly evolved over time, so we can call it by a name and address it separately. The truth of the matter is that the fluidity of the medium of games is such that it is hard to pinpoint when a genre truly ends and another begins, but regardless of what we call them there is no denying that the social games as they exist now are very different from what we used to call social games in the past. My intention when writing this book was to highlight the incredible amount of knowledge about player behaviour and

DOI: 10.1201/9781003314325-15

virtual social structures that can be derived from these kinds of games. Regardless of your area of expertise, I hope my insight into how people use these kinds of games I have helped create has contributed to painting a more fully fledged picture of the "social gamer" that goes beyond the stereotypical preconceived notion of them.

I believe there are many ways to impress readers in order to gain credibility. We can throw around numbers in an attempt to get people's attention and convince them that what we have to say is not only important but in some way revolutionary. My intention here however was not to talk about success but rather to present our discoveries that are less so about specific game design tenants or mechanics as they are about the behaviours observed in the audience when interacting with said mechanics. And even though this is an area of game development that feels very specific, the lessons we learned about the audience speak more broadly about the users of modern ways of communication. These users we have observed and I have described in this book are also more than just a case study for specific demographic preferences, instead I believe them to be heralds of trends that are starting to emerge. They speak to the different aspects of our lives online and how the blend of real and digital is slowly but surely happening.

It's essential to always remember that in design nothing is one size fits all. Whether we are going from the mainstream into a specific area or if we are taking knowledge from a niche into the mainstream, tailoring the experience to the audience we have is the most important. Testing out ideas and understanding your audience is not a point that can be skipped in my opinion. If there is any lesson that I would suggest anyone can take and use in their games is that the games of the future are a lot more fluidly developed than we have been used to developing so far. They involve a great degree of player psychology and player involvement, and we as developers need to have a clear understanding of the purpose the game serves in people's lives beyond just the surface desire to entertain. Especially when we look at games as social catalysts and want to explore their ability to create and maintain bonds, it's important to remember how the design of a product affects its use and how we then end up playing a role in people's social lives.

References

Resources

Ballantine, Paul W., and Brett A. S Martin. "Forming Parasocial Relationships in Online Communities." Edited by Geeta Menon and Akshay R. Rao. *NA – Advances in Consumer Research*, vol. 32, 2005, pp. 197–201. Association for Consumer Research. https://www.acrwebsite.org/volumes/9073/volu-. Accessed 10 November 2023.

Birdwhistell, Ray L. *Introduction to Kinesics: (An Annotation System for Analysis of Body Motion and Gesture)*. Department of State, Foreign Service Institute, 1952. https://books.google.co.uk/books?hl=en&lr=&id=Ad99AAAAMAAJ&oi=fnd&pg=PA2&dq=Ray+Birdwhistell'%E2%80%99s+work+on+Kinesics+in+the+1950s&ots=xm8zO49dxk&sig=9TAqBoYWrSU3ohLudJ6bGTlt9zs&redir_esc=y#v=onepage&q=Ray%20Birdwhistell%E2%80%99s%20work%20on%20Kinesics%.

Böcking, Saskia. "Suspension of Disbelief." Edited by W. Donsbach. *The International Encyclopedia of Communication*, 2008. https://doi.org/10.1002/9781405186407.wbiecs121.

Bogost, Ian. "The Rhetoric of Video Games." *The Ecology of Games: Connecting Youth, Games, and Learning*. Edited by Katie Salen. Cambridge, MA: The MIT Press, 2008. https://www.gunkelweb.com/coms465/texts/bogost_rhetoric.pdf. Accessed 9 November 2023.

Boudreau, Kelly. *Between Play and Design: The Emergence of Hybrid-Identity in Single-Player Videogames*. Université de Montréal, 2012. https://papyrus.bib.umontreal.ca/xmlui/bitstream/handle/1866/8713/Boudreau_Kelly_2012_these.pdf.

Boudreau, Kelly, and Shanly Dixon. "Playing With Social Network Sites: Actual & Ideal Selves." *Selected Papers of Internet Research*, vol. 14, 2013, n/a.

Caillois, Roger. *Man, Play, and Games*. Translated by Meyer Barash. Free Press of Glencoe, 1961.

Dixon, Stacy Jo. "U.S. Facebook User Activities 2020." *Statista*, 28 April 2022. https://www.statista.com/statistics/275788/share-of-facebook-user-activities/. Accessed 11 November 2023.

Ellemers, Naomi, et al. "Self and Social Identity." *Annual Review of Psychology*, no. 53, 2002, pp. 161–186. https://d1wqtxts1xzle7.cloudfront.net/65962258/Self_and_Social_Identity20210310-13766-mazek6.pdf?1615390257=&response

-content-disposition=inline%3B+filename%3DS_Elf_and_S_Ocial_I
_Dentity.pdf&Expires=1699377347&Signature=c21O2GgRQlcAOFYfDkD
YHuAnIR7VvFHsaY1B. Accessed 7 November 2023.

Frasca, Gonzalo. *The Video Game Theory Reader*. Edited by Mark J. P. Wolf and Bernard Perron. Taylor & Francis Group, 2013.

Goffman, Erving. *Frame Analysis: An Essay on the Organization of Experience.* Harvard University Press, 1974.

Hall, Edward T. "Proxemics [and Comments and Replies]." *Current Anthropology*, vol. 9, no. 2/3, 1968, pp. 83–108. https://www.jstor.org/stable/2740724?origin =JSTOR-pdf&seq=1.

Huizinga, Johan. *Homo Ludens ILS 86*. Taylor & Francis Group, 2014.

Jensen, Graham H. "Making Sense of Play in Video Games: Ludus, Paidia, and Possibility Spaces." *Eludamos. Journal for Computer Game Culture*, vol. 7, no. 1, 2013, pp. 69–80. https://septentrio.uit.no/index.php/eludamos/article/view /vol7no1-4/7-1-4-pdf.

Kahneman, Daniel. *Thinking, Fast and Slow*. Farrar, Straus and Giroux, 2012.

Kannengiesser, Udo, and John S. Gero. "Design Thinking, Fast and Slow: A Framework for Kahneman's Dual-System Theory in Design." *Design Science*, vol. 5, 2019. Cambridge University Press. https://www.cambridge.org/core /journals/design-science/article/design-thinking-fast-and-slow-a-frame- work-for-kahnemans-dualsystem-theory-in-design/A200DC637BBDC98 2D288FC4F8A112DE7#. Accessed 12 November 2023.

Kumari, Ruchika, and Rachana Gangwar. "A Critical Study of Digital Nonverbal Communication in Interpersonal and Group Communication: In Context of Social Media." *International Journal of Communication and Media Studies (IJCMS)*, vol. 8, no. 4, 2018, pp. 1–12. https://www.researchgate.net/profile /Rachana-Gangwar-2/publication/362453109_A_CRITICAL_STUDY_OF _DIGITAL_NONVERBAL_COMMUNICATION_IN_INTERPERSONAL_ AND_GROUP_COMMUNICATION_IN_CONTEXT_OF_SOCIAL_MEDIA /links/62ea9a2288b83e7320a67730/A-CRITICAL-STUDY-OF-DIGITAL-. Accessed 15 November 2023.

Mcleod, Saul. "Maslow's Hierarchy of Needs." *Simply Psychology*, October 2023.

Power, Thomas G. *Play and Exploration in Children and Animals*. Taylor & Francis, 1999.

Rathore, Ashish K., et al. "Social Media Content and Product Co-creation: An Emerging Paradigm." *Journal of Enterprise Information Management*, vol. 29, no. 1, 2016, pp. 7–18. https://www.emerald.com/insight/content/doi/10.1108 /JEIM-06-2015-0047/full/html.

Rogers, Everett M. *Diffusion of Innovations*. Free Press of Glencoe, 1962.

Rubin, Jason. "Changes to the Instant Games Platform." *Facebook*, 2020. https:// www.facebook.com/fbgaminghome/blog/changes-to-the-instant-games -platform. Accessed 11 November 2023.

Shand, John. *Central Works of Philosophy V2: Seventeenth and Eighteenth Centuries.* Edited by John Shand. Taylor & Francis, 2015.

Shaw, Adrienne. "Do You Identify as a Gamer? Gender, Race, Sexuality, and Gamer Identity." *New Media & Society*, vol. 14, no. 1, pp. 28–44. https://www .ctcs505.com/wp-content/uploads/2016/01/Shaw-2012-Do-you-identify-as -a-gamer.pdf.

Sherry Jr., John F. "Gift Giving in Anthropological Perspective." *The Journal of Consumer Research*, vol. 10, no. 2, 1983, pp. 157–168. https://www.research-gate.net/profile/John-Sherry/publication/24098336_Gift_Giving_in_Anthropological_Perspective/links/540764690cf2bba34c1f0fc9/Gift-Giving-in-Anthropological-Perspective.pdf.

Statista. "UK Facebook Users by Age Group 2023." *Statista*, 22 May 2023. https://www.statista.com/statistics/1030055/facebook-users-united-kingdom/. Accessed 11 November 2023.

Statista. "U.S. Facebook User Activities 2020." *Statista*, 28 April 2022. https://www.statista.com/statistics/275788/share-of-facebook-user-activities/. Accessed 11 November 2023.

Stone, Douglas, and Sheila Heen. *Thanks for the Feedback: The Science and Art of Receiving Feedback Well: (Even When It Is Off Base, Unfair, Poorly Delivered, and Frankly, You're Not in the Mood)*. Portfolio Penguin, 2014.

Suciu, Peter. "Gen Z Not 'Friending' On Facebook – How Will the Social Network Respond?" *Forbes*, 6 September 2022. https://www.forbes.com/sites/peter-suciu/2022/09/06/gen-z-not-friending-on-facebookhow-will-the-social-net-work-respond/. Accessed 11 November 2023.

Tam, Charles. *The Royal Game of Ur*. 2008. https://mitocw.ups.edu.ec/courses/comparative-media-studies-writing/cms-608-game-design-spring-2008/projects/tam1.pdf.

Venkatesan, Soumhya. "The Social Life of a 'Free' Gift." *Journal of the American Ethnological Society*, vol. 38, no. 1, pp. 47–57. https://www.researchgate.net/profile/Soumhya-Venkatesan/publication/230091227_The_Social_Life_of_a_Free_Gift/links/59d2225ca6fdcc181ad5e412/The-Social-Life-of-a-Free-Gift.pdf.

Wood, Natalie T., and Michael R. Solomon. *Virtual Social Identity and Consumer Behavior*. M.E. Sharpe, 2009.

Yee, Nick. *The Proteus Paradox: How Online Games and Virtual Worlds Change Us—And How They Don't*. Yale University Press, 2014.

Yee, Nick, and Jeremy Bailenson. "The Proteus Effect: The Effect of Transformed Self-Representation on Behavior." *Human Communication Research*, vol. 33, no. 3, 2007, pp. 271–290.

Zastrow, Mark. "Is Video Game Addiction Really an Addiction?" *Proceedings of the National Academy of Sciences*, vol. 114, no. 17, 2017, pp. 4268–4272. National Academy of Sciences. https://www.pnas.org/doi/epdf/10.1073/pnas.1705077114. Accessed 11 November 2023.

Games

Among Us, Innersloth, 2018.

Candy Crush Saga, King, 2012.

City of Heroes, Cryptic Studios, and Paragon Studios, 2004.

Coin Master, Moon Active, 2015.

Counter Strike: Global Offensive, Valve, and Hidden Path Entertainment, 2012.

Dark Pictures Anthology, Supermassive Games, 2019.

Destiny 2, Bungie, 2017.

Diplomacy, Allan B. Calhamer. Wizards of the Coast, 1959.

Don't Starve Together, Klei Entertainment, 2014.

Doom, id Software, 1993.
Dungeons & Dragons, Gygax, Gary, and Dave Arneson. 1 ed., 1974.
Eve Online, CCP Games, 2003.
FarmVille, Zynga, 2009.
Fortnite, Epic Games, and People Can Fly, 2017.
Gardenscapes: New Acres, Playrix, 2016.
Gartic Phone, Onrizon, 2020.
Gauntlet, Atari Games, 1985.
Genshin Impact, miHoYo, and Shanghai Miha Touring Film Technology Co., Ltd., 2020.
Guild Wars, ArenaNet, 2005.
Guild Wars 2, ArenaNet, 2012.
Harvest Moon, Amccus, 1996.
Hay Day, Supercell, 2012.
HQ, Intermedia Labs, August, 2017.
Keep Talking and Nobody Explodes, Steel Crate Games, 2015.
Microsoft Solitaire, Microsoft, 1990.
Minecraft, Mojang Studios, 2009.
Minesweeper, Microsoft, 1989.
Monopoly, Phillips, Elizabeth J. Magie, and Charles Darrow, 1933.
Monster Hunter, Capcom, 2004.
Mortal Kombat, Boon, Ed, and John Tobias, 1992.
Pokémon GO, Niantic, Inc., 2016.
Pong, Atari Games, 1972.
Ragnarok Online, Gravity, 2002.
Second Life, Linden Lab, 2003.
Stardew Valley, ConcernedApe, 2016.
Street Fighter, Capcom, 1987.
StreetPass Mii Plaza, Nintendo, 2011.
Super Mario Land, Nintendo, 1989.
Tetris, Pajitnov, Alexey, 1986.
Terraria, Re-Logic, 2011.
The Settlers of Catan, Teuber, Klaus, and Catan Studio. 5 ed., 2015.
Until Dawn, Supermassive Games, 2015.
Words with Friends, Zynga, 2009.
World of Warcraft, Blizzard Entertainment, 2004.
YoVille, Big Viking Games, and Zynga, 2008.
Yu-Gi-Oh!, Konami, 2002.
Zynga Poker, Zynga, 2007.

Index

Printed in the United States
by Baker & Taylor Publisher Services